# SIMPLE PRINCIPLES™
# TO ENJOY LIFE AND BE HAPPY

Alex A. Lluch
**Author of Over 3 Million Books Sold!***

Dr. Helen Eckmann
Doctor of Education and Leadership Science

WS Publishing Group
San Diego, California

SIMPLE PRINCIPLES™
TO ENJOY LIFE AND BE HAPPY

By Alex A. Lluch and Dr. Helen Eckmann

Published by WS Publishing Group
San Diego, California 92119
Copyright © 2008 by WS Publishing Group

Designed by WS Publishing Group:
David Defenbaugh

For Inquiries:
Logon to www.WSPublishingGroup.com
E-mail info@WSPublishingGroup.com

ISBN 13: 978-1-934386-05-7

Printed in China

# TABLE OF CONTENTS

# INTRODUCTION

Happiness is one of the most sought-after states of being on the planet; yet what does it mean to be truly happy? In many ways, being happy is the culmination of many other states of being, such as feeling calm, pleasure, satisfaction, and joy. Being happy includes walking around with a smile on your face, savoring the day you just had, and looking forward to tomorrow.

The best thing about happiness is that there exists an infinite supply. We need only to tap into the various sources within us to raise our level of positivity. At the same time, we must quell the negativity that tends to creep within us. In other words, the key to being happy is to balance the internal scale that measures out doses of positive or negative feedback and reactions.

Everyone wants to lead a full life complete with loving

relationships, satisfying work, and an overall sense of happiness. So why is it so hard for many of us to be happy? Our world is increasingly violent, sad, stressful, and fast-paced. Happiness can be a hard-to-find emotion in the midst of such an environment. This book arms you with tools to make you a happier person no matter what your circumstances are. These tools, or coping skills, are essential to deal with stress, crises, tragedies, triumphs, and life changes.

So much of our unhappiness is due to the fact that we are constantly reacting instead of being proactive. If you are constantly flustered, you will live in a state of high adrenaline, tension, and stress. You can control all of these adverse reactions by changing the way you think, feel, and behave. Having control over your life is different from being a controlling person, however. Trying to control people and elements causes only frustration and misery. Learning to manage your own emotions and responses, on the other hand, is fundamental to your success and happiness. Motivational speaker Tony Robbins once said, "The secret of success is learning how to use pain and pleasure instead of having pain and pleasure use you. If you do that, you're in control of your life. If you don't, life controls you." Reading this book is a very important first step in getting control of your life and increasing your happiness.

## What is this book about?

In short, this is a book about being happy. In more depth, this is a book about accepting who you are, developing a healthy outlook, and honing faith and values. It is about learning new skills, including forgiveness, being happy for others, anger management, and how to cope with sadness. This book also offers information on how being a more generous and charitable person can increase your happiness, and why nurturing your relationships, developing a sense of purpose, and overcoming fear will make you a happier person. Finally, this book is about maximizing your health, self-esteem, and environment to result in a more fulfilling, more productive, and happier you. Use this book as a tool to help you lead a happier life.

It's important to remember that life is a series of ups and downs. Society tells us that the only life worth living is a happy one, but if we didn't know sadness, we couldn't know happiness. Sadness is necessary for happiness to exist. It's impossible to be 100 percent happy, and that's okay.

This book shows you how to improve your self-esteem by changing what you can and by accepting what you cannot change, such as your gender or race. Many people are surprised to find that the capacity to lead a happier life is completely within their control.

This book emphasizes the role that positive thinking plays in your overall happiness. Several simple principles included in this book guide you away from negative self-talk. There are principles to help you learn how to change your mind about your abilities and circumstances.

**Who should read this book?**

This book is for people who want to:
- Learn to accept their flaws
- Learn to capitalize on their strengths
- Figure out how having faith fits into their overall happiness
- Explore what their core values are

- Learn to forgive others—and themselves
- Avoid feelings of jealousy
- Get control of their anger
- Incorporate charity into their lives
- Take care of their physical and mental health
- Learn tools for coping with sadness
- Learn to nurture their relationships
- Practice relaxation and stress-reduction techniques
- Overcome fear and anxiety
- Set goals and find their purpose
- Boost their self-esteem
- Learn how environment affects happiness
- Give themselves permission for "me time"
- Develop and maintain a positive outlook

Lastly, this book is for people who want to be able to flip to a page in a book that applies to their situation and find an inspirational tip that will quickly put them on the path to happiness.

## Why should you read this book?

Well, there is a reason why you were drawn to the title. But the fact is that everyone should read this book. Even if you consider yourself to be a happy person, there is something in here for you. You should read this book because it combines lots of wisdom into easy-to-read simple principles. If you want to change your life and be a much happier person, you should read this book. Here are some questions to ask yourself:

- Are you tired of hanging on to old resentment, but aren't sure how to purge it?
- Do you become easily frustrated?
- Do you feel guilty when you make time for your own needs?
- Is it difficult for you to celebrate others' successes?
- Are you a slave to "always" and "never"?
- Is it impossible for you to relax?
- Have you lost someone you loved?
- Are you satisfied with your relationships?
- Does fear prevent you from trying new things?
- Do you think obsessively about your flaws?

- Is your life without direction?
- Do you blame your parents for your unhappiness?
- Do you have a problem finding enjoyment with life?

These are just a few of the many topics covered in this book. If any of these questions resonate with you, read on. The principles contained in this book are researched and supported with inspirational quotes and statistical information from credible sources. Its size makes it easy to keep with you for easy reference or for a quick pick-me-up in the middle of the day. You should read this book whenever you are ready to make some changes and improve your overall outlook on life.

# HAPPINESS
## IN THE MODERN WORLD

Americans today have higher incomes, and the ability to buy more stuff. We have remote controls to turn our TVs on and off, to open our garages, and to control our lights, ceiling fans, and indoor temperatures. Aging is easier, and we're living longer. We are more educated than any other generation, and travel is often affordable and convenient. We can find the answer to just about anything in few seconds by using the Internet. We can call anyone, anytime, on our cell phones, and send emails from anywhere.

Yet despite all these advantages, Americans report the lowest level of happiness among citizens of any industrialized country. According to reporter John Lanchester in an article from *The New Yorker* magazine, "Looking at the data from all over the world, it is clear that, instead of getting happier as they become better off, people get stuck on a 'hedonic treadmill': their expectations rise at the same pace as their incomes, and the happiness they seek remains constantly just out of reach."

So, we have more, we do more, and we're in constant communication. But there clearly exists a disconnect between how we live and our level of happiness.

**Why is it so difficult to be happy?**

Humans are emotional creatures whose ideas of happiness are constantly changing. What made you happy as a teenager is not the same as what satisfies you as an adult. Yet many of us do not update our goals and desires. It is recommended that you evaluate your goals once a day to make sure they continue to reflect where you are in life. How many of us do this even once a week?

Keeping up with the world around you is also key to your level of happiness. Your ability to adapt to our changing world will equip you with the tools you need to be successful. Consider the difference between an elderly person who keeps up with the times — learns how to use email, and therefore is in close contact with his family and able to receive digital pictures, etc. — and an elderly person who chooses not to participate in modern communication methods. One feels included and in the know, while the other feels isolated and alone. Senior citizens who are "connected" to society report a much higher level of happiness, which translates into better overall health.

Surviving our materialistic and expensive culture is another key to happiness. Indeed, the environment in which we live puts tremendous weight on material gain. What if you can't afford to keep up with the latest trends? Is it a struggle to feed, clothe, or house your family? Many Americans must work overtime or get a second job to make ends meet. Financial strain is the number one reason people cite for why they are unable to be happy. Body image is a close second. According to *BBC News*, "More than 70 percent of women had made serious attempts to diet in the last year and 58 percent had 'disordered' eating patterns." We abuse ourselves to fit in when life would be so much easier if we could just accept our flaws and celebrate our strengths. Reading the following simple principles will start you on the path to self-acceptance, which is necessary to experience true happiness.

**What do you need to begin the pursuit of happiness?**

This book offers the following tools to help you pursue happiness in your life:

- Methods to practice positive thinking
- Ideas on how to let go of resentment
- Exercises that teach self-esteem
- How to replace negative thoughts with positive thoughts
- Ideas for spending quality time with yourself
- How to accept your flaws
- How to accentuate your strengths
- Ways to explore your faith
- The beauty and freedom in forgiveness
- The negative toll jealousy takes on your relationships
- The connection between your physical and emotional health
- The benefits of generosity
- The importance of giving time to the people you care about

This book also will teach you that:

- Your perspective is everything
- Learning to cope with sadness does not devalue your loss
- Controlling your stress directly affects your ability to be happy
- Fear inhibits happiness
- Having a sense of purpose is key to giving your life meaning
- Low self-esteem is the cause of most unhappiness
- Our environment affects your outlook
- Time spent on yourself is time well spent
- Having a positive outlook takes work

Use the simple principles in this book as you would a toolbox. Refer to them often as you need to and practice feeling happier. Eventually the tips and practices recommended in this book will become second nature.

**How will I know when I am happy?**

Achieving happiness is a process. You will know that you are making progress when you feel happy more often than not. If you feel in control of your life, you are in good shape. When replacing negative self-talk with affirming messages becomes second nature it is a good indicator that you are happier than you were before.

# Maximizing the Benefits of This Book

Always keep this book handy. Put it in the glove compartment of your car. Stick it in the top drawer of your desk at work. Lay it on your night stand before bed. This book was written to be read over and over again. The principles will take time to affect change, so read and practice them often. Remember that your pursuit of a happier life is a journey that will take commitment and effort. However, you will feel better almost immediately once you start reading this book.

# ACCEPTING WHO YOU ARE

We are all born without judgment. An infant doesn't know if he is black, white, blind, or even whether he is able to move all of his limbs. It is precious when children do not understand what makes them different from one another. But as we grow up, the world tends to shuttle us into various categories, grouping us by what we can or cannot do, what we look like, and where we come from. In this way, our environment comes into play as a key component in our happiness. Think about the environment in which you were raised: In what type of household did you grow up? What television shows did you watch? Were there people like you in the books you read? All of these things influence how you regard yourself. Throughout your life media, family, school, and other influences taught you to view yourself as different from others. Too often, these differences are perceived as flaws or limitations.

In truth, all human beings are flawed. Each of us has qualities that we cannot change. Accepting those parts of you that cannot be changed is a critical part of becoming a happier person. Once you are able to accept who you are, you can stop spending energy wondering why you are not someone else or pitying yourself for being different. In time, you will realize the things about yourself that cannot be changed are not flaws. Rather, they are special qualities that make you unique and extraordinary.

George Orwell wrote, "Happiness can exist only in acceptance." If you long to be happier, you must work to accept who you are at this moment. The following principles will help you come to terms with the things about yourself that you cannot change—your family, ethnicity, physical or emotional differences. They will help you understand that the parts of you that cannot be changed must be incorporated into a whole and beautiful, imperfectly perfect you.

# Principle #1

## Minimize how many times a day you think about your flaws.

———————— ✳ ————————

How much energy do you waste dwelling on your flaws? Take note how many times you think, "I hate _____ about myself." You will likely be surprised at how often you single out your most undesirable qualities. Instead of living in a constant state of remorse about things you cannot change, try modifying the messages you tell yourself. Start by thinking, "If I can't change this, I'm going to embrace it." Instead of fighting your flaws, accept them as part and parcel of who you are.

# PRINCIPLE #2

## Focus on the things that you have or can do.

❋

Complaining about things that are out of your control and cannot be changed is counterproductive. Rather than dwelling on what you lack or cannot do, focus on what you can do. Highlighting your abilities will enable you to see a way forward, whereas "I can't" statements force you to focus on obstacles. As the American poet James Whitcomb Riley once quipped, "It is no use to grumble and complain; it's just as cheap and easy to rejoice. When God sorts out the weather and sends rain—Why, rain's my choice." When you cannot change something, highlight the part of you that can move forward.

# PRINCIPLE #3

## Don't just survive: thrive!

People face more horrors in life than can be imagined. Every day, men, women, and children survive abuse, disaster, catastrophe, violence, sickness, and loss. Being traumatized after any upsetting event is natural and to be expected. But living through a tragedy is also a feat worth celebrating. Those who overcome a tragedy yet continue to live in survival mode limit their ability to truly live. Therefore, it is important to come away from tragedy by celebrating the fact that you are alive. You will never be able to undo the event that traumatized you, but you can spend the rest of your life not merely surviving, but thriving.

# PRINCIPLE #4

## Stylize your crutch.

The actress Anna Lee once said, "They see me wheeling around in a beautiful gown, and they realize you can look elegant, and you can lead a happy life in a wheelchair." Instead of being embarrassed of the tools you rely on to get through life, work them into your personality. If you wear glasses, choose a pair that suits your face. If you use a wheelchair to get around, add flair to your chair. If you walk with a cane, choose a beautifully carved one, or add a funny knob that reflects your personality. Just because you use a crutch does not mean it must be dull or embarrassing.

# Principle #5

## Turn your limitation into your greatest strength.

An empowering way to become happy with who you are is to turn your limitation into a skill, asset, or trademark. Famous examples of those who turned their limitations into strengths include the famous cyclist Lance Armstrong who became an advocate for cancer research after he survived testicular cancer. Similarly, actor Michael J. Fox, who suffers from Parkinson's disease, has worked tirelessly to bring attention to the disease. In doing so, he has become a household name synonymous with strength, courage, and perseverance. Become a leader in your community and show others that your limitation is also your greatest strength.

# Principle #6

## Forgive your parents for their mistakes.

———————— ✳ ————————

Oscar Wilde once wrote, "Children begin by loving their parents; after a time they judge them; rarely, if ever, do they forgive them." Indeed, too many of us walk through life resenting our parents for the mistakes they made. But as adults, we must realize that children do not come with an instruction manual. Odds are your parents did the best job they could in the era in which they lived and with the resources available to them. Blaming your parents for your shortcomings will not help you overcome them. Instead, find solace in the good family memories you do have.

# Principle #7

## Own your flaws, don't let them own you.

Each of us has something we cannot change. Instead of letting that quality defeat you, present it as something that makes you unique and special. For example, you may feel frustrated that you are shorter than you would like to be. There is little you can do to increase your height, but you can change the way you carry yourself. Make platform shoes your signature fashion piece; speak loudly and clearly in order to be seen as a person of stature and importance. You will be much happier once you own your size, shape, and abilities with pride instead of trying to be someone different.

# PRINCIPLE #8

## Recognize racism is a sickness you alone cannot cure.

For all of the different races, ethnicities, and religions, the sad truth exists that there are many people who hate blindly. If you are the victim of a racist or otherwise hateful act, do not blame yourself for someone else's sickness. Think instead of what historian Pierre Berton said of racism: "Racism is a refuge for the ignorant. It seeks to divide and to destroy. It is the enemy of freedom, and deserves to be met head-on and stamped out." Counteract the racist and hateful acts you witness by becoming a spokesperson for peace, tolerance, and love.

# Principle #9

## Be yourself, not what other people expect you to be.

Each of us is a member of some race, gender, ethnicity, religion, or other group. Such membership offers solidarity and a sense of identity, but it can also come with an expectation to be like everyone else in that group. Do not be afraid to maintain your individuality by rejecting what does not match up with who you are. Similarly, do not feel pressure to be an ambassador for your race, gender, ethnicity, or religion. Demand that others treat you as an individual and do the same for them.

# PRINCIPLE #10

## Shake up gender roles by doing the unexpected.

❊

Even in the 21st century, gender roles continue to shape behavioral expectations for men and women. But no one should be herded toward certain duties or qualities simply because of their gender. Learn the exhilaration that can come from pushing the traditional gender-role boundaries. Men may want to take a night to plan and cook dinner for their family; women may choose to spend a Saturday afternoon attending to a home-improvement project. Defying gender roles can open doors to new opportunities and interests at work, home, and in the community.

# Increasing Faith and Values

Think of the happiest people you know. If you ask the secret to their contentment, they would probably tell you that their happiness stems from faith. Indeed, faith plays an integral role in happiness — but why? For one, faith provides answers where there seem to be none. On the contrary, the faithless come up short for answers all the time. For example, many of us spend much of our lives trying to figure out why bad things happen to good people. Why does the young girl with no family history get cancer? Why does the thief live to be 90 while a good-hearted, generous person has their life cut short too soon? There is often no clear reason for such injustices, so having faith that everything happens because it fits into a grand plan is exceptionally comforting.

Believing in a grand plan and in something larger than you will help put life's setbacks and disappointments into perspective and may even improve your health. Studies repeatedly show that people with faith who suffer from life-threatening ailments recover faster and live longer than those who do not have faith. In fact, *The New York Times* had this to say about the healing property of faith: "In a study of 232 elderly patients who had undergone open-heart surgery, those who were able to find strength and comfort in their religious outlook had a survival rate three times higher than those who found no balm in religious faith."

Belonging to an organized religion or having a sense of spirituality can also help establish and strengthen your values and derive a sense of right and wrong. By cultivating a set of standards to live up to, such as being a good, generous, decent person, they are more likely to treat family, friends, and even strangers with respect and kindness. Through religious and spiritual practices, they develop a sense of responsibility and respect for history, fellow humans, and the environment.

Use the following principles to refresh your sense of faith and articulate a set of values that you believe are important for living. The principles will show you that even in the darkest times, faith can help you find your way back to happiness.

# Principle #11

## Learn to have faith.

Faith can be a supporting pillar of happiness. But too often, people try and force themselves to have faith because their family, friends, or community leaders push them into it. To truly be a person of faith, avoid approaching faith from a place of guilt. Instead of thinking, "I should believe this because my religion says I have to," make your faith personal. Don't believe in something simply because someone else does or tells you to. Decide for yourself the things that you believe and stay true to them.

# PRINCIPLE #12

## Practice what you preach.

—— ✳ ——

Your values make up your own personal code of conduct. Therefore, it is important to practice what you preach. If you espouse "love thy neighbor," then you must treat your neighbors with love and kindness. Following your own rules and being true to the values you believe are important is self-affirming. Most assuredly, it will make you a better and happier person.

# Principle #13

## Have faith in a higher power when you are down and out.

———————— ✳ ————————

An old proverb states, "Fear knocked at the door. Faith answered. And no one was there." Indeed, there is no more important time to have faith than when you are filled with fear, doubt, and sorrow. Faith can conquer each of these demons. So look to the sky when all you can see is the ground. Turn your head up and feel that you are not alone. It is during your most difficult times that you most need your faith, so keep your head up and feel God's comforting presence.

# Principle #14

## Understand that everything happens for a reason.

———— ✳ ————

Perhaps one of the most frequently asked questions in the world is, "Why did something bad happen to such a good person?" Indeed, all the major religions have focused much of their creeds on attempting to answer this question, which in religious circles is known as *theodicy*. There is often no clear reason for injustice, so at times we must simply have faith that everything happens for a reason. Albert Einstein said about God, "I am convinced that He does not play dice."

# PRINCIPLE #15

## Take part in religious traditions.

Holidays are times for joy and celebration in large part because of the traditions we share with friends and family. Upholding your religious traditions is an important part of your heritage and identity. Studies show that people who are tied to their family through ritual and faith have higher self-esteem and an overall sense of well-being. When we let our traditions falter, we often feel empty and purposeless. Stay connected to your past by upholding your family's traditions and teaching them to your children.   They are an integral part of who you are and who your children will become.

# PRINCIPLE #16

## Believe that there is a God.

———————————— ❋ ————————————

If you struggle with your faith, you are not alone. In one study of religious and spiritual people, more than 80 percent admitted to doubting that God exists at some point. But part of being human is experiencing periods of doubt and confusion. If your faith falters now and then, remind yourself that while no one can prove there is a god, no one can prove there isn't. Then, err on the side of faith for a more meaningful and happy existence. As Morris West once shared, "Once you accept the existence of God, however you define him, then you are caught forever with his presence in the center of all things."

# PRINCIPLE #17

## Believe in a grand plan.

Martin Luther King Jr. once likened faith to climbing a staircase in spite of not being able to see every step. Indeed, putting your trust in the existence of a grand plan is difficult at times, but important. Humans have an inherent need to organize chaos. One way to approach the chaos of life, death, tragedy, and joy is to believe in a grand plan that is the destination to which all individual lives lead. Finding meaning through believing in such a grand plan will help alleviate spiritual crises and bring meaning and purpose to your life.

# PRINCIPLE #18

## Follow the Ten Commandments, and add to them.

No matter what religion you practice, the basic ethical principles summarized in the Ten Commandments are good rules by which to live an honest and happy life. This is why all the world's major religions incorporate these basic tenets in some way. Honoring your parents and spouse; promising not to steal, lie, cheat, and murder; and being a good neighbor are principles everyone should strive to live up to. Feel free to tailor the idea of commandments by adding principles that are especially important to you, such as, "I will be kind to animals," or "I will respect the environment." Principles such as these echo the Ten Commandments by demonstrating love for the weak and honoring God through stewardship of the earth.

# PRINCIPLE #19

## Don't be afraid to believe in what cannot be proven.

Many people struggle because faith requires them to accept ideas that cannot be proven. But never let anyone tell you that having faith is a mark of unintelligence. In fact, according to Planet Project, a polling company that surveyed 380,000 people in more than 225 countries, highly educated people are more likely to believe in God. Of those polled, 63 percent of those who said they believed in God had a secondary-school education, while 72 percent of believers held a college degree.

# PRINCIPLE #20

## Live a clean and honest life.

The satisfaction and emotional peace that comes from living an honest life is hard to rival. Lies, on the other hand, poison your good intentions and prevent you from living a clean and free life. Lies also cause you to feel guilty, and guilt festers. Living in the shadow of these burdens causes severe physical and emotional stress. Always tell the truth even when it is difficult to do so. Living with lies is highly self-destructive and will prevent you from ever being deeply happy.

# LEARNING HOW TO FORGIVE

One of the biggest challenges you will face in your quest for a happier life is learning how to forgive. People mistakenly believe that if they forgive someone who has harmed them, they approve of the offensive behavior. But this is not so. If you forgive someone who steals from you, it does not mean that you agree that stealing is an acceptable behavior. It simply means you accept the reality of the situation and want to move forward to better and more productive things.

Additionally, forgiving is not necessarily something you do for the benefit of someone who has wronged you. First and foremost, forgiving is a process that is for your own personal benefit. Walking around with anger and resentment is extremely unhealthy; such a weight can drain us more than we realize.

Therefore, learning how to forgive is a way to lighten your load. Life is difficult enough; adding years of collected resentments on top of normal responsibilities will keep you facing backwards, waiting for justice for past wrongs. When you forgive someone who stole from you, you release the resentment toward the thief that unhealthily burdened you. This does not mean that you must forget the event. It simply means you set yourself free from the negative feelings associated with the person who wronged you. It was for this very reason that theology professor Lewis B. Smedes wrote, "To forgive is to set a prisoner free and discover that the prisoner was you."

Though it takes a great deal of emotional work to forgive, it is worth it. Your mental, physical, and emotional health will improve when you no longer feel the need to hold on to grudges, hurts, and wrongs. The following principles will teach you how to both ask for and receive forgiveness. As psychotherapist Robert Karen writes, "True forgiveness isn't easy, but it transforms us significantly. To forgive is to love and to feel worthy of love. In that sense, it is always worthwhile."

# Principle #21

## Realize that forgiveness is a process.

"Forgive and forget" is not as easy as it sounds. A Gallup poll that surveyed Americans on the topic of forgiveness found that 94 percent believed it is important to forgive, but 85 percent said forgiveness is something they are unable to do without help and work. There are three steps that often work to achieving forgiveness. First, you must acknowledge your feelings by letting the person know that he or she hurt you. Second, tell the person who offended you that their words or actions were unacceptable. Third, be prepared to accept an apology. Do not rush any of these steps, and take solace in the fact that forgiveness is a difficult and slow process for most of us.

# Principle #22

## Don't be afraid to say you're sorry.

—— ❋ ——

When someone tells you that you've hurt their feelings, listen intently. Fight the urge to become defensive. Don't get bogged down in the details of the event. Instead, focus on what you did or said that was hurtful. Take responsibility for your words and actions, be humble, and apologize. A heartfelt apology can go a long way in healing a wounded relationship. Apologizing when appropriate will also free you from guilt and shame, which are major obstacles to happiness. Through this process, you will obtain personal growth, strength of character, and the respect of others.

# Principle #23

## Control your anger.

A natural response to being wronged is anger. However, consider the situation beyond your own perspective. For example, if your wallet was stolen, think about whether the thief was hungry and desperate. Or, perhaps someone hit your car and failed to leave a note — could he have been rushing a child to the hospital? Since your wallet may not be returned and you will never learn who hit your car, it makes little sense to hang on to resentment. Realizing you have been a victim of circumstance can help you to forgive. As the founder of Buddhism, Siddartha Gautama, said, "Anger will never disappear so long as thoughts of resentment are cherished in the mind."

# Principle #24

## Do not hang on to resentment.

Too many of us hang on to resentment and allow it to become who we are. But it is important to let go or else our biggest wounds may become our foremost identity. Learn to drop your identity as the victim and replace it with something healthy and inspiring. Instead of being the "guy whose wife left him," become the guy who is amazing because he forgave his ex-wife. You were a whole person before you became attached to your wounds. Become more than your pain by returning to that state of wholeness.

# PRINCIPLE #25

## Practice forgiveness.

Alexander Pope wrote, "To err is human; to forgive, divine." Most religions teach the need for forgiveness and yet it is one of humanity's biggest challenges. Unforgiveness often stems from our desire to be right and our tendency to turn experiences of injustice into opportunities for self-pity. These behaviors will derail your happiness over and over again. As Pope points out, we each have the ability to perform a divine act by forgiving those who have harmed us. Be divine and forgive. You will feel better about yourself and be closer to God.

# Principle #26

## Experience the freedom that forgiveness brings.

— ❈ —

Theology professor Lewis B. Smedes has written, "To forgive is to set a prisoner free and discover that the prisoner was you." Bearing these ugly feelings is extremely unhealthy, and can cause chronic health and emotional problems. Lighten your load by learning how to forgive. This does not mean that you must forget the event. It simply means you set yourself free from negativity, resentment, and anger. Feeling free is one of the many keys to being a more joyful person.

# PRINCIPLE #27

## Always forgive your enemies.

— ✳ —

Oscar Wilde put it best when he said, "Always forgive your enemies — nothing annoys them so much." Take the power away from the person who caused you harm by forgiving him. By living in the shadow of a hurtful event, you allow someone to dictate your identity. Instead, take satisfaction in being the bigger person. Aim to inspire those around you — especially your enemies — with your capacity for generosity and forgiveness. This is a surefire way to make those who have wronged you feel ashamed of their actions, and thus truly sorry.

# PRINCIPLE #28

## Apologize when you have done something wrong.

Most relationships become stronger after an argument that ends with a heartfelt apology. For this reason, American poet Bryan H. McGill has noted, "There is no love without forgiveness, and there is no forgiveness without love." Both receiving and offering an apology can help reinstate lost confidence in a partner, friend, or coworker. Strong relationships are built on trust, which comes from knowing that people can take responsibility for themselves and also graciously accept flaws in others. Therefore, accept or give a deserved apology to further enforce the bonds between you and the people you care about.

# PRINCIPLE #29

## Give and accept forgiveness.

Researcher Everett Worthington Jr. is just one scientist who has concluded that people who forgive others have better overall health, stay married longer, and have more friends, which leads to a happier life. Conversely, angry people are not at peace, because they are obsessed with what went wrong instead of what can be made right. Carrying around your bag of grudges will not bring you any closer to becoming a happier person. To achieve true peace and happiness, integrate the practice of forgiving and being forgiven into your life. The apostle Paul wrote in his letter to the Ephesians, "Do not let the sun go down on your anger."

# PRINCIPLE #30

## Know the difference between forgiving and accepting mistreatment or abuse.

※

Forgiving someone for abusing or mistreating you is not the same thing as accepting the behavior. Forgiveness is more about building a stronger future that benefits from overcoming mistakes of the past. It was with this knowledge that Dutch physician Paul Boese remarked, "Forgiveness does not change the past, but it does enlarge the future." If someone in your life repeatedly makes the same mistakes, however, it is time to consider whether they are worthy of being forgiven. Do not let your ability to forgive be an invitation for someone to take advantage of you.

# PRINCIPLE #31

## If you forgive, truly do so.

So you have forgiven your sister for spilling red wine on your wedding dress. Or have you? The answer is "no" if you bring it up at every family event and use it as a weapon each time you have an argument. Once you decide to forgive, you must make a commitment to let go of the event — or else you haven't truly forgiven. Instead of telling the "ruined wedding dress" story every Thanksgiving, talk about the touching toast your sister gave. Your sister will appreciate being let off the hook and you will have successfully forgiven her.

# Principle #32

## Forgive yourself.

Perhaps the most difficult person to forgive is yourself. Too often we are our own worst critics, our meanest enemies, our harshest judges. In fact, a University of Michigan study found that an incredible number of Americans — 44 percent of men and 43 percent of women — are unable to forgive themselves. However, the study also found that people able to forgive themselves are more satisfied with their lives and less likely to report symptoms of psychological distress, feelings of nervousness, restlessness, and sadness. While it is important to hold yourself to high standards, it is equally important to forgive yourself in order to move forward with a happier, healthier life.

# CHANGING YOUR PERSPECTIVE

We have all heard the phrase, "Happiness is a state of mind" — but what does this phrase really mean? To be human is to think and our thoughts shape our perspective. In turn, our perspective determines our interpretations, actions and reactions, and, essentially, makes us who we are and how we feel.

Though it may not always feel like it, each of us controls our thoughts, and therefore our outlook. Keeping negative thoughts to a minimum and replacing them with positive ideas is a critical step on the road to happiness. There is no more powerful tool available to a person than his thoughts. It was because of this reality that Abraham Lincoln once said, "Most folks are about as happy as they make their minds up to be."

The benefits of positive thinking are well-studied and

plentiful. Researchers have concluded that people who have an optimistic perspective tend to live longer and healthier lives than those who are pessimistic. Some health benefits of positive thinking are reduced stress, higher resistance to the common cold, easier breathing, stable heart rate, and lower blood pressure — to name just a few. Studies also show that people who have a positive perspective tend to make healthier choices, such as eating well and avoiding the urge to overindulge in alcohol or drugs.

People who lean toward positive thinking also tend to have better coping skills in times of hardship. Coping is difficult when faced with a tragedy, but when you add messages such as "I will never get through this," you train your brain to expect a negative outcome, which adversely affects your ability to handle life's challenges. Instead, tell yourself, "I can handle this. I will be okay." Even if you don't believe it at first, you will grow into the idea, and the act of telling yourself you will be okay can greatly help the situation. Use the following principles to reinforce these messages and to learn other ways to develop a perspective that increases your level of happiness.

# Principle #33

## Fill your day with positive thoughts.

Insert positive thinking into your daily routine in the same way you brush your teeth, eat meals, and change your clothes. When you wake, think of the things in life you are thankful for. Focus on the events and tasks you most look forward to doing that day. Plan to do things you know will give you pleasure and joy, even in small amounts. When settling down at night, review the parts of your day that made you most happy. If it was a bad day, concentrate on the things you will do tomorrow to make it better.

# PRINCIPLE #34

## Focus on what is right in your life.

———————— ❄ ————————

An old Swedish proverb states, "Worry often gives a small thing a big shadow." Indeed, we make mountains out of molehills by needlessly obsessing over things that are imperfect in our lives. Resist the urge to fixate on what you want to change about yourself or your circumstances. Instead, focus on what is working in your life, and channel your energy into those areas. Affirming the good aspects of life allows them to flourish and gives you energy to improve other areas that may need more attention.

# Principle #35

Smile often — even when
you don't feel like it.

Even if you don't feel like it, smile. It can make you feel better. Smiling releases endorphins, natural pain killers produced by the brain. In addition, put positive thinking behind your smile; a 2005 study by the Wake Forest University Baptist Medical Center found that thinking positively actually helps people overcome pain. In fact, Dr. Tetsuo Koyama, the lead author of the study, said, "Positive expectations produced about a 28 percent decrease in pain ratings — equal to a shot of morphine." So smile — it is a simple way to change the way you feel from the outside in.

# Principle #36

## The here and now is a gift given to you by your past.

Dr. Norman Vincent Peale, author of the influential book *The Power of Positive Thinking*, summed up the importance of starting fresh each day in the following way: "Yesterday ended with last night." Indeed, it is important to release yourself from yesterday's mistakes. See each new day as a chance to start with a clean slate. Consider past failures as wisdom in the making rather than defining elements of who you are. Practice imagining the present as a gift you get to open anew every day.

# PRINCIPLE #37

## Believe in possibilities!

Being optimistic is not only key to being a happy person but also key to living a long and healthy life. According to one medical study published in the journal *Archives of General Psychiatry*, optimistic patients have a 55 percent lower risk of death from all causes and 23 percent lower risk of death from heart failure. The ability to look on the bright side, therefore, can translate into not only a happier life but a longer one. The next time you feel inclined to think negatively about a situation, focus your efforts instead on picturing yourself in a better place, and believe in the possibility of getting there.

# Principle #38

## Incorporate positive affirmations into your daily routine.

Positive thinking does not often come naturally. Many people must train themselves to view things in a positive light. Use positive affirmations to reprogram negative thoughts. Instead of telling yourself, "I will never be happy," think, "I am happy at this moment." Over time, the moments will add up to a powerful collection of positive hours, and eventually, days. Not only will affirming the positive give you higher-quality days but more of them; a recent study by researchers at the Mayo Clinic found that people who think positively live 19 percent longer than those who do not.

# Principle #39

## Use visualization techniques to improve your outlook.

In 2006, Rhonda Byrne's book *The Secret* became a bestselling book overnight. But the book's main premise is no secret at all. According to *The Secret*, the key to happiness and success is to picture yourself as a happy and successful person. Use visualization techniques to achieve this. For example, write yourself a check for a million dollars and stick it on your bathroom mirror. Look at it every day. This will not only encourage you to seek out lucrative opportunities but will remind you of your worth. This and other visualization techniques can help you build a positive outlook.

# Principle #40

## Keep a journal of things you enjoy and do a few of them every day.

The way we view things is a by-product of our daily experiences. We all have positive experiences every day but many of us concentrate on our negative ones. For one week, keep a list of positive experiences. No enjoyment is too small to record. For example, take note if you tried a new flavor of coffee you enjoyed or found a shortcut that reduces your commute by 10 minutes. At the end of the week, notice how many little joys life presented, and be sure to repeat them.

# Principle #41

## Learn to love the person in the mirror.

According to Planet Project, a global Internet polling company that polled 380,000 people in more than 225 countries, just 35 percent of all people enjoy the view when they look in the mirror. That means when 65 percent of the world's population looks in the mirror, they are disappointed! Improve your outlook by enjoying what you see. Look in the mirror each morning and find something about yourself that pleases you. Say, "I have lovely eyes," or "I like the way my hair looks today." After a while, you will learn to love the whole image.

# Principle #42

## View setbacks as opportunities.

Henry Ford once said, "The world was built to develop character, and we must learn that the setbacks and grieves which we endure help us in our marching onward." The father of the assembly line and the Model T automobile was no stranger to setbacks. As an inventor, he repeatedly hit roadblocks that stalled his progress. But Ford always turned setbacks into opportunities. His reward was crafting a variety of successful inventions that over his lifetime won him 161 U.S. patents. Think of Ford the next time you hit a roadblock. Viewing setbacks as opportunities rather than obstacles is foundational to developing a positive outlook and becoming a happy person.

# BEING HAPPY FOR OTHERS

Jealousy is recognized as one of the ugliest human emotions. People who use jealousy as their primary way of dealing with others will never be able to be fully happy. If you are a jealous person, you are likely trapped by anger, fear, hatred, and loneliness. It is not possible to be happy when consumed by these feelings.

There are two main types of jealousy. The first is covetous in nature — when you want what another person has. Most of us have felt jealous of another person at some point, and this is normal to a degree. However, if you are so unhappy in your own life that you find it impossible to feel happy for others, then jealousy is a serious problem for you that must be overcome.

The second type of jealousy is when you find it impossible to share your partner or friends with anyone else. The inability to trust your partner with others, and the insistence on being included in events to simply keep an eye on him or her stems largely from insecurity. Alexander Berzin, an expert in Tibetan Buddhist traditions, explains, "If we are insecure, then when a friend or partner is with someone else, we are jealous. This is because we are unsure of our self-worth, insecure of the other person's love for 'ourselves,' and thus we do not trust."

Jealousy causes you to become unattractive to your partner, friends, family, and coworkers. Left unchecked, jealousy will lead you to become sneaky and obsessed with catching others in what you perceive to be betrayals. This paranoid and accusatory behavior can destroy both your self-esteem and your relationships.

To overcome jealousy, first identify what type of jealousy you suffer from. Taking stock of the good and unique things in your own life is one way to avoid feeling jealous of what others have. If you are jealous of the time your partner spends with colleagues or friends, assure yourself that you will not so easily be forgotten or replaced by others. Most importantly, realize that overcoming jealousy is a difficult but necessary task in order to be a happier person. The following principles will teach you how to incorporate being happy for others into your everyday life.

# Principle #43

## Focus on feeling content in your own life.

The majority of Americans suffer from jealousy, according to a groundbreaking study published in the *Journal of Personality*. Interestingly, researchers found that when people were asked what percent of the general population were jealous, they estimated 75 percent, but only 54 percent labeled themselves as jealous people. If you struggle with jealousy, concentrate on centering yourself within your own life. Focus on what you like about your situation — your job, your friends, your home, your hobbies. There is nothing to be gained from lamenting what is lacking. Instead, take stock of what you do have and be thankful for it.

# Principle #44

## Don't compare your life to someone else's.

Comparing your life to another person's is like comparing dogs and cats or jeans and corduroy. Because everyone is so different, you are bound to come up short in some area. Interestingly, siblings are especially likely to compare their lives in detrimental ways. A study published in the *Journal of Family Communication* found that 52 percent of all people experience a jealousy incident within their family. Comparing your life with family members and others will cause you to feel unnecessarily incomplete. Avoid this common pitfall and compare yourself only to your own past and present.

# PRINCIPLE #45

## A perfect forest is made up of imperfect trees.

From a distance, a forest looks beautiful and perfect. Upon closer inspection, you will see that some of the trees are bare, some are rotten, some are diseased, and some have fallen. Remember that each person looks like a perfect forest, and that you cannot see the various and damaged trees that make up the whole grove. When you find yourself feeling jealous of another person's life, try to remember that everyone has flaws that cannot be seen. You'll feel better once you can ground yourself in the reality that perfection is only in the eye of the beholder.

# Principle #46

## Reacting with jealousy steals someone else's special moment.

———————— ✳ ————————

Few of us intentionally want to take away another person's special moment. However, if you make a cutting remark and express jealousy when your friend announces an engagement, promotion, or raise, you steal the beauty of your friend's moment. He or she only gets one chance to make that first announcement. Be supportive and truly happy for others — they will be truly happy for you when it is your turn to announce special news.

# PRINCIPLE #47

## Acknowledge feelings of jealousy but don't dwell on them.

You should never ignore or deny an emotion, especially one as powerful as jealousy. Feel it, acknowledge it, but let it pass. Letting jealousy sit without processing it can cause adverse health reactions such as heart palpitations, high blood pressure, and poor digestion. The author William Penn once insightfully noted, "The jealous are troublesome to others, but a torment to themselves." Don't torture yourself with feelings of jealousy. Everyone gets jealous now and then — allow yourself to do so, and then move on to more productive emotions.

# PRINCIPLE #48

## Don't waste time on jealousy.

---- ❊ ----

Time is constantly moving forward — you cannot go back, so avoid spending irreplaceable moments obsessing over others' possessions or luck. How many minutes have you wasted wishing you had your neighbor's new car or wishing you could have your friend's seemingly perfect kid? As author Mary Schmidt once advised, "Don't waste time on jealousy. Sometimes you're ahead, sometimes you're behind." Staying present in your own life is a surefire way to be happy in it.

# Principle #49

## Love yourself.

Psychologists say that low self-esteem is the number one cause of jealousy. If you do not feel worthy of another person's affections or friendship, you may try to control what they do and with whom they spend their time. This behavior is damaging to all relationships, but especially to your relationship with yourself. Trust that you are worth the love and affections of others — start by loving yourself.

# Principle #50

## Rejoice in other people's success.

Practice being the first to congratulate a friend who receives something you wanted for yourself. This is the best way to take power away from ugly feelings of jealousy or insecurity when something good happens to someone else. Instead of asking internally, "Why didn't this happen to me?" say out loud, "I'm so happy for you!" You may not mean it at first, but with practice, you will.

# Principle #51

## Do not obsess over the good fortune of others.

Scholar Harold Coffin once remarked: "Envy is the art of counting the other fellow's blessings instead of your own." Indeed, it is infinitely damaging to your well-being to obsess over the good fortune of those around you and fail to see your own. This type of thinking tends to divide the world into winners and losers, a world view which often leads to "poor me" thinking. Such self-pitying overshadows all of your wonderful qualities and dwells on what is probably not true about you. In life, everyone both wins and loses some of the time, including you.

# PRINCIPLE #52

## Realize things are seldom what they seem.

The British playwright Lawrence Durrell once observed, "It is not love that is blind, but jealousy." Indeed, jealousy obscures our ability to see clearly. Before you waste energy wishing you were in your sister's seemingly perfect marriage or had your friend's seemingly perfect family, realize that things are seldom what they seem. Perfection is an unobtainable illusion. Though a marriage may appear perfect, you can never know what truly goes on behind closed doors. Similarly, your friend's parents may visit more often than yours but the visits may be less than perfect. Just because things appear a certain way does not mean you would want them if you understood their reality.

# Principle #53

If you are not happy about something, do something about it.

There is nothing to be gained by jealously fixating on what someone else has and wishing you could have that too. Instead, turn jealous energy toward being proactive and goal-oriented to achieve your own dreams. Know the things that you like, the things that make you happy, and focus on them. Don't assume that what makes those around you happy will be the things that fulfill you as well.

# PRINCIPLE #54

## Learn to trust people.

It is difficult, yet important, to surround yourself with trustworthy people. It is believed that the word "jealousy" derives from the French word for Venetian blinds, which is *jalousie.* Psychiatrist Nils Retterstol suggests that a husband observed his wife from behind a *jalousie* and caught her in the act of adultery. The reality is that, more often than not, the people you jealously guard would not betray you to begin with. Even if they plan to, your jealousy will not likely stop them from doing so. Therefore, resign yourself to leading a jealousy-free life; you truly have nothing to lose and a lot to gain.

# Managing Anger

Happy people are not angry people. But all of us feel angry from time to time. Anger is a normal response to an upsetting situation. Everyone experiences some form of anger. The key to managing anger is to find healthy ways to express it.

Imagine yourself as a tea kettle. Your normal range of emotions causes the water inside to warm up and cool down. When you are really angry, the water will boil, and the kettle even whistles a warning. To silence the whistle and cool the water, you must take off the lid and let off some steam. Regularly doing so will prevent boiling over or inappropriate outbursts.

People who successfully manage their anger report low incidence of depression and dissatisfaction. Anger management requires that you spend time relaxing every day. This will promote an overall sense of calm. Controlling outbursts requires that you change the way you react when you are angry. Instead of throwing your keys on the ground and cursing when your car won't start, learn to take deep breaths to calm yourself. Finally, realize that out-of-control anger hurts you the most. A Korean proverb states, "If you kick a stone in anger, you'll hurt your own foot." Indeed, outbursts of uncontrollable and unjustifiable anger will quickly alienate you from friends, family, and coworkers.

It is important to express your anger — just be mindful of how you do it. According to the American Psychological Association, unexpressed anger will lead you to become pessimistic and difficult to be around: "People who are constantly putting others down, criticizing everything, and making cynical comments haven't learned how to constructively express their anger. Not surprisingly, they aren't likely to have many successful relationships."

It is said that for every minute you are angry you lose 60 seconds of happiness. Unexpressed and unmanaged anger prevents you from achieving happiness. The principles in this chapter teach you how to calm yourself and express feelings in a healthy way. After all, you cannot prevent others from angering you, but you can control your response.

# Principle #55

## Express anger before it turns to rage.

Everyone feels angry every now and then, but what separates a normal person from a person with an anger problem is being able to express it in a healthy way. A Buddhist proverb states, "Holding on to anger is like grasping a hot coal with the intent of throwing it at someone else; you are the one who gets burned." Indeed, holding on to anger and collecting things to be angry about quickly leads to unhappiness, which only hurts you. It is a good idea to deal with small annoyances as they come up rather than wait until you explode with rage.

# Principle #56

## When you are tense, take a deep breath.

———————— ✳ ————————

When you feel anger coming on, take deep breaths that start low in your belly. Exhale until every drop of breath has left your lungs. This type of deep, rhythmic breathing expands the diaphragm, the muscle located below your lungs. This type of breathing allows you to take in more oxygen and release more carbon dioxide with each breath. Deep breathing promotes more oxygen flow to your brain and lymphatic system. Deep breathing releases endorphins, the body's natural pain killers and relaxants. When you are angry, deep breathing will ease you into a state of physical calm, and your mood will surely follow.

# Principle #57

## Avoid road rage.

Inappropriate anger can get us into dangerous, even life-threatening, situations. Indeed, a 2006 *Sunday Times Magazine* report found that more than 80 percent of drivers have been involved in road rage incidents and 25 percent have committed an act of road rage. Remind yourself that flying into a rage endangers you and others. A way to avoid becoming angry would be to imagine yourself or someone you love in a car accident, or worse, in the hospital because of a rash and angry act while driving. Prevent such a scene from becoming a reality by keeping your cool at all costs.

# Principle #58

## Avoid using "never" and "always" during an argument.

Avoid making blanket statements during the course of an argument. Exclaiming "You're always late!" or "You never listen to me!" is not only inaccurate but inflammatory. Using "always" and "never" also serves to make you think your anger is justified, when really it is an exaggeration of the facts. Keep your cool and speak only to the specific situation in front of you. Being fair and accurate when you express grievances to others will win you the respect of the people you disagree with and might possibly lead to reconciliation.

# Principle #59

## Stay calm during an argument.

The playwright Wilson Mizner once wrote, "The worst-tempered people I've ever met were people who knew they were wrong." Indeed, anger clouds our judgment and tends to weaken, rather than strengthen, our position in an argument or discussion. Anger feeds irrational thought, and an irrational person is neither respectable nor believable during the course of an interaction. By emotionally detaching from the situation, you may then use logic, rationality, and facts to win your arguments, not anger.

# Principle #60

## Focus on how to solve a problem and not the problem itself.

———————————— ✳ ————————————

Will Rogers famously noted that "people who fly into a rage always make a bad landing." So too will you if you let anger get in the way of solving a problem. It is frustrating to come up against problems, but you are likely to solve them more quickly and efficiently if you keep your cool. Getting angry clouds your ability to think clearly and prevents you from coming up with ways to cope. Instead, take a minute to think of realistic steps that can fix the problem. Focus your energy on dealing with life's challenges effectively rather than angrily.

# PRINCIPLE #61

## Funny faces keep you from angry places.

Humor is often our best defense against becoming a raving lunatic. When you feel yourself heading toward a tantrum, make a funny face in the mirror. If appropriate, make a joke when fighting with another person to show that, although anger is a serious emotion, you do not take yourself too seriously. Laughing will make both of you feel better almost immediately. Do avoid sarcasm or jokes at another's expense, however, as this just expresses anger in nonproductive ways.

# Principle #62

## Make your environment anger-resistant.

———————— ✳ ————————

If your house is making you crazy because you are too busy to clean it, step outside, go for a walk, and revisit the mess when you feel better able to tackle it. Staring down a sink full of dishes after a full day of work and fighting traffic on your way home is a disaster waiting to happen. Keep your surroundings manageable so when you are spread thin, toys in the middle of the room or similar clutter won't tip your scales from irritation to full-blown anger.

# Principle #63

## Only small, petty people are ruffled by small, petty events.

Journalist Sydney J. Harris once asked, "If a small thing has the power to make you angry, does that not indicate something about your size?" Indeed, only small, petty people are ruffled by small, petty events. Show those around you the depth of your character by refusing to become undone by minor obstacles. Also, prevent anger by avoiding circumstances that will lead to frustration. Map a new route to work if your current one is heavily trafficked. Find a new lunch spot if you can no longer stand listening to your coworkers complain. In as many ways as possible, create a success-prone and stress-free environment for yourself.

# PRINCIPLE #64

## Don't fight just to be right.

---- ✳ ----

Many of us will argue long into the night just to prove we are right. Such battles are to be avoided at all costs. Those who appear overly argumentative and stubborn are seldom admired or respected. If you cannot convince someone of your opinion within a few calm exchanges, simply defuse the conversation by agreeing to disagree. Chances are, someone who is willing to go round after round with you will never be convinced to see it your way anyway.

# Principle #65

## Adopt a "who cares" attitude.

❋

The next time you are tempted to lose your cool, try reacting with a "who cares" attitude. If the bottom of your grocery bag rips, spend a minute laughing at the situation. If there is a line at the bank, make conversation with the person ahead of you. If you make a wrong turn, find a good song on the radio to pass the extra time. People are inspired by those who appear joyous, carefree, and happy. Being carefree and untroubled, on the other hand, is emblematic of someone who is young at heart and delights in life.

# PRINCIPLE #66

## If you can't get control of your anger, get counseling.

Some people have a chronic anger problem that needs professional attention. If this is your case, seek counseling. Therapy can help you get to the root cause of your anger and teach you techniques to both express and control your emotions. Letting anger go unchecked at this level is unhealthy and can become dangerous. At least one certified anger management professional can be found in most major cities. Seek out the one nearest you and begin treatment if you still can't control your anger after reading and implementing the suggestions found in this book.

# Helping Others

An old proverb states, "When you dig another out of their troubles, you find a place to bury your own." There is no surer path to becoming a happier person than to help others.

Charity has been a key feature of the world's major religions for centuries. Jews give 10 percent of their earnings to charity. In fact, *tzedakah*, the Hebrew word for charity, is considered one of the highest of all obligations and is one of three acts required by Jews in order to receive God's forgiveness. Christianity has the concept of *tithing*, which requires Christians to give 10 percent of the household income to the church. Likewise, *zakat*, or almsgiving, is one of the Five Pillars of Islam. Muslims are supposed to give part of their income to those who are less fortunate.

Even if you do not belong to a particular religion, consider practicing charity as a social duty. Generosity has always been a backbone of society, but our culture increasingly tends to keep people focused on self-preservation. This environment causes us to feel disconnected from one another. People who volunteer their time once a week, on the other hand, feel valued and needed. This improves health and builds self-esteem, which leads to feeling happy, purposeful, and complete.

Offering your time and resources helps shift your focus from your own problems to the needs of others and puts things into perspective. It is a positive way to incorporate generosity and charity into your life.

Taking care of those who are less fortunate benefits both the giver and the receiver. You are able to have a positive impact on someone else's life, and you get to feel good about yourself. Volunteering enhances your résumé and also enables you to show gratitude for help you may have received in the past.

Use the principles that follow to discover ways to become a more charitable person. You will feel happier when you are bringing joy to the lives of others.

# Principle #67

## Volunteer your time.

Anne Frank wrote in her famous diary, "How wonderful it is that nobody need wait a single moment before starting to improve the world." There are many levels at which you can volunteer. Investigate the charitable programs in your area. Perhaps you can serve meals at a church once a month, or tutor homeless children at the local shelter. The time you give to others is often as valuable to them (or more so) as money. Giving your time to a worthy cause also helps put your own problems in perspective, gives you a sense of belonging within a community, and enhances your sense of self-worth.

# Principle #68

## Donate a percentage of your earnings to charity.

Not everyone has time to give, and that's okay. If this is your situation, consider donating a percentage of your annual income to charity. This is an easy, effortless way to give back to society. Writing a check or pledging to your favorite charities can be a satisfying and enjoyable experience, as economists in the UK found after conducting a study in which a group of women were each given $100 to donate to charities. Researchers noted that after their donation, brain scans on the women showed increased activity in the area of the brain that registers pleasure.

# Principle #69

## Someone else needs what you are about to throw away.

Spring cleaning? Call your local charity! Many agencies will even come to your home to pick up your discarded treasures. Clothes, shoes, toys, furniture, housewares, and other items are often in high demand at homeless shelters and thrift stores who sell items to support the agencies that own them. Even if the item feels small or trivial, donate it rather than throw it away. Not only will this benefit the charity, the earth will benefit as well, as the item will avoid the landfill. As the philosopher Edmund Burke once said, "Nobody made a greater mistake than he who did nothing because he could only do a little."

# Principle #70

## Compliment a stranger.

Imagine you are sitting in your doctor's office, agitated because he is running late. The woman across from you says, "Excuse me, I just had to say that you have a great haircut! Who is your stylist?" Odds are that you will feel the agitation melt away and enter a discussion that lifts your spirits. Do this for one person each day and chances are you will elevate another person's mood as well as your own.

# Principle #71

## Do favors for your friends.

Friends are wonderful gifts and they should be rewarded now and then for their friendship. If you know a friend is moving, offer to help box up his belongings. Or house-sit while your pal goes on a much-needed vacation. Make dinner for a friend and surprise her with it when she gets home from a rough day at work. The way to have a great friend is to be one. You will both benefit from these small kindnesses.

# Principle #72

## Organize a food drive.

———————————— ✻ ————————————

Everyone should be able to eat three meals a day but, unfortunately, many people go without. The National Coalition for the Homeless estimates there are as many as 3.5 million homeless in the U.S., 39 percent of whom are children. Surveys by the Coalition and partner organizations found that 40 percent of homeless go at least one day a month with nothing to eat. You can help those less fortunate than you by incorporating a food drive into your holiday traditions. It can be as simple as setting out a box in your store or office, collecting canned and dry goods, and dropping them off at a local charitable organization or shelter.

# Principle #73

## Small acts of kindness reap big rewards.

Let the person with just a gallon of milk go ahead of you in the check-out line. Give up the prize parking space at the mall to the woman who has two kids in the back seat. Put your neighbor's newspaper on his porch when it looks like it is going to rain. Allow the driver next to you to enter your lane. Living in a constant state of "me first" causes aggression, anger, and tension; however, studies show people who practice small acts of kindness on a daily basis are less stressed and feel better about themselves than the "me first" set.

# PRINCIPLE #74

## Become a pen pal.

———— ❋ ————

There is great value in receiving a handwritten letter, especially in a world where hundreds of emails are thoughtlessly dashed off per day. Sitting down to write a letter can be therapeutic for you and very meaningful to the recipient. Consider writing to a soldier overseas, a prisoner, or an elderly person in a nursing home. Pen Pals for Soldiers (www.penpalsforsoldiers.org), Prison Fellowships (www.prisonfellowship.org), and Pen Pal News (www.writeseniors.com) are good places to go for more information on embarking on a new relationship via paper and pen.

# Principle #75

## Buy products that support your favorite charities.

It may take some investigating, but many companies donate a portion of their profits to various charities. For example, Working Assets, a telephone and credit card company, donates money to various charities. They have donated $50 million since 1985 to organizations that promote peace, economic justice, and education. Similarly, since 1991, the Discover credit card company has donated more than $14 million in scholarships to needy students. Purchasing products from companies that financially support charities is a good and simple way to practice generosity.

# Principle #76

## Give blood to your local blood bank.

— ❄ —

Less than 5 percent of healthy Americans eligible to donate blood actually do so. According to Blood Centers of the Pacific, the need for blood is great — on any given day, approximately 34,000 units of blood are needed to treat accident victims, people undergoing surgery, and patients receiving treatment for leukemia, cancer, or other diseases. If your health permits it, donate blood often. In times of natural disasters or other crises, feel proud you have done your part to ensure your community is prepared for the worst.

# Principle #77

## Teach your children to be generous.

Teach your child to share and be generous at an early age. Involve your child in your charitable activities, perhaps bringing your son or daughter along to a Habitat for Humanity project or to feed the hungry at a soup kitchen. Ask your children for ideas on how to help kids less fortunate than they are. You will be surprised to hear how simple yet perfect kids' thoughts can be on helping others. Doing charity together cultivates a common interest with your child that can be nurtured throughout life.

# Principle #78

## Use your influence to help someone else.

———————— ✳ ————————

There are many ways to use your influence to help others. Pass a friend's résumé along to your boss (as long as he or she is qualified). Did you witness an accident or a crime? Notify the police and tell them what you saw. If you notice a person taking advantage of someone less capable, step in and help. For instance, if you notice that a merchant is overcharging an elderly person, point out the actual price and help with the transaction. Appropriately intervening on behalf of others will make you feel capable and important.

# Taking Care of Your Health

Too many of us do not see the connection between our physical health and our happiness until the body breaks down. It then becomes a huge undertaking to reverse the ill effects of our neglect. Let this chapter serve as your wake-up call to commit to living a healthier — and thus happier — lifestyle.

Studies show that poor diet and inactivity lead to conditions such as obesity, headaches, diabetes, and cancer. A sedentary lifestyle decreases energy levels and dulls memory and concentration. Chronic poor health eventually leads to high blood pressure, irregular heartbeat, and depression. So, how can you avoid becoming depressed as a result of poor health?

Begin keeping a food journal. Log everything that you eat and drink for 5 days. You will be able to notice dietary problems and where you are lacking in nutrition. Start by adding fresh fruits and vegetables, lean protein, and whole grains to your meals. Avoid excessive consumption of alcohol, which is a depressant. High caffeine and sugar consumption will cause you to crash in the afternoon and become irritable. Quitting smoking now greatly reduces your risk for lung, throat, and other smoking-related cancers.

Keep your body in shape with daily exercise. Taking care of your own health should be a top priority. According to the Centers for Disease Control, more than 50 percent of Americans do not engage in enough exercise to see improvements to their health. Make sure you get at least 30 minutes of exercise several times per week. Engaging in frequent exercise will improve your mood in as little as 2 weeks. You will find that the more time you spend being active the better you will feel, and the more you will want to stay active. This will lead you to a place of contentment, health, and happiness.

Exercise is just one way to improve your health and therefore increase your happiness. The following principles will show you other ways to conquer common health problems in order to overcome obstacles to your happiness.

# Principle #79

## Get enough sleep.

There are many studies that show that lack of sleep increases stress and heart rate as well as decreases coordination and metabolism. Getting at least 8 hours of sleep every night is important to your overall well-being. So grab that extra sleep when you can! Skip the morning news and sleep in or put down that novel and go to bed early. Avoid tossing and turning over what has been left undone by taking care of pressing tasks before you go to bed. If you feel too tired to attend to everything before you sleep, write down a list of those things that need your attention and let them go; trust yourself to accomplish them tomorrow.

# Principle #80

## Eat less more often.

For energy-filled, positive days, eat 6 small meals every day instead of 3 large ones. Eating smaller, more frequent meals will increase your metabolism and keep insulin levels even throughout the entire day. Waiting too long between meals teaches your body to "save up" fat and shift into starvation mode to conserve energy. This can slow your metabolism and make you feel lethargic. Dan Benardot, professor of nutrition, kinesiology, and health at Georgia State University explains why eating small meals every 3 hours is best to raise energy and mood levels: "Blood sugar fluxes every 3 hours, so if you don't eat something to raise the blood sugar, metabolic rate can slow down."

# Principle #81

## Limit caffeine and sugar intake.

According to Johns Hopkins University School of Medicine, 80 to 90 percent of North American adults and more than 165 million Americans report using caffeine regularly. In fact, caffeine is the world's most commonly used drug. When you feel yourself crashing and need a lift, avoid reaching for caffeine and sugar. Instead, give yourself a natural boost by eating a light, healthy snack such as yogurt, nuts, or fruit. Re-up your energy by taking a brisk walk or stretching. There are many ways to reenergize without the harmful and negative after-effects of overindulging in caffeine and sugar.

# PRINCIPLE #82

## The right foods improve your moods.

Scientific studies have repeatedly found a strong connection between food and mood. Incorporate complex carbohydrates like fruits, vegetables, and whole grains into your diet. Each of these help maintain levels of serotonin, a mood-elevating chemical in the brain. Nutritionist Susan Kleiner explains the connection between food and mood in the following way: "It's what anti-depressants are all about. These drugs work to elevate serotonin levels or at least keep them from dropping too low. The right foods accomplish the same thing."

# Principle #83

## Avoid activities that trigger overeating.

Have you ever experienced remorse after bingeing on chips and cookies while watching hours of television? Identify the activities that trigger overeating for you and avoid or limit them. If you plan to watch a long movie, be sure to have a healthy snack on hand. Air-popped popcorn and dried fruit are great alternatives to the sugar- and calorie-laden junk food that is usually associated with watching television or movies.

# PRINCIPLE #84

## Learn the art of meditation and deep breathing.

❋

Meditation quiets the mind, which enables you to concentrate and think clearly for longer periods of time. Research shows that meditation also increases cardiovascular and respiratory health as well as boosts the immune system. One study followed the health of more than 2,000 people over a 5-year period. Researchers found that those who meditated had more than 50 percent fewer doctor visits than did non-meditators of similar age, gender, and profession. To optimize your health, carve out just 15 minutes each day to be quiet with your thoughts and practice deep breathing.

# Principle #85

## Limit your alcohol intake.

———————————————————— ✳ ————————————————————

Enjoy a glass of wine with dinner or an ice-cold beer at a summer barbecue — but don't overdo it. Remember, alcohol impairs your ability to think and function. Alcohol also prevents your liver from breaking down sugar, which turns into stored fat and leads to a "beer belly" or "wine tire." Although a second glass of wine may feel good at the time, the next day you may feel sluggish or hungover, which will cause you to be unprepared for work and other planned engagements. Remember, alcohol is a depressant, so use it sparingly.

# Principle #86

## Moving your body gives you a natural high.

Be sure to get at least 30 minutes of physical activity every day. Many of us think we are too busy to exercise, but you should always make exercise a priority in your schedule. Try using half of your lunch break to go for a brisk walk after your meal. Or, take a walk around your neighborhood before or after dinner. When you exercise, your body releases endorphins, which naturally elevate your mood and give you more energy. Take advantage of the benefits of exercise, in some form or another, every day.

# Principle #87

## Stretch to improve your quality of life.

Stretching has many health benefits: it increases flexibility and can be used to rev up your body before starting your day or help you to wind down at night. Research shows that people who stretch have fewer back problems, are less prone to injury, and are able to work longer and play harder than those who let their muscles tighten with age and inactivity. Stretching can also rid the body of built-up stress and tension, which will help you sleep more peacefully.

# PRINCIPLE #88

## Hydrate your way to happiness.

The human body is made up of more than 50 percent water. Everyday activities such as sweating during exercise cause the body to lose water, which must be replenished. Drinking water will bring down your body temperature when you are too hot. Also, the number one way to prevent your skin from aging prematurely is to consume plenty of water—at least 8 glasses per day. Finally, choose water over sugary sodas or juices in order to keep yourself hydrated without taking in unwanted calories.

# Principle #89

## Quit smoking right now.

───────── ✳ ─────────

Quitting smoking greatly reduces your risk for developing respiratory ailments, heart disease, and smoking-related cancers. It can take 10-14 days to get over the initial discomfort of nicotine withdrawal, but enduring two weeks of withdrawal is worth improving your health for years to come. Former smokers consistently testify that they are happier than when they smoked. In fact, a poll taken by the American Cancer Society found that 85 percent of former smokers wished they had quit at least 5 years earlier than they did. Not only are their clothes, hair, and breath free of the smell of cigarettes but they are less socially isolated as well because they quit smoking.

# Principle #90

## Have an annual physical.

There's an easy way to monitor your health — see your doctor for your annual physical. Sadly, many of us avoid the doctor. Men are particularly avoidant; a 2000 survey by The Commonwealth Fund, the country's largest public affairs forum, found that 1 out of every 3 men do not have a regular doctor, and 1 out of 4 said he would wait as long as possible before getting treatment if he felt sick or was worried about his health. Be proactive and choose disease prevention over healing after the fact. Knowing you are healthy will bring you peace of mind, instill a sense of well-being, and promote happiness.

# Coping with Sadness

No book on how to live a happier life would be complete without addressing the reality of occasional sadness in our lives. Coping with sadness is a challenge many of us face daily to varying degrees. Learning to cope with sadness *before* you are faced with a major loss will prepare you for surviving sadness and enjoying other aspects of life.

Learning how to cope with separation, death, and health problems is a necessary part of living. This chapter will teach you the steps to relieve your heavy heart from some of its sadness. First, though, you must assess whether you are momentarily sad or more seriously depressed. If you are depressed, realize that this is not an uncommon state of mind. But you shouldn't allow chronic depression to go untreated. Instead, see a doctor or therapist, because you may need a professional to help guide you. If you are experiencing a disproportionate level of sadness due to a particular event, you will recover and find happiness again if you take care not to let your sadness spiral out of control.

There are many ways to manage your sadness. Share your feelings with trusted friends or family members. Keep a journal and record your thoughts on what happened and how you are processing it. Remember the good things in your life and nurture them. Continue to take care of yourself, even when coping is hard. Let yourself have a good, cathartic cry now and then. Continue to engage in activities you enjoyed before becoming sad. Keep yourself busy, but remember to give yourself time to acknowledge your feelings and then let them go. Philosopher Kahlil Gibran once wrote, "Sadness is but a wall between two gardens." In this spirit, use the following principles to remember who you were before your tragic event took place and allow them to show you how to be happy again.

# Principle #91

## Mourn when your loss is fresh.

When a loved one dies, many of us go into "survival" mode. Things need to be done, so we do them. It may seem like as long as you keep moving and doing, you will be okay. This state of autopilot might carry you through the initial shock but can lead to a crushing collapse as time passes on. So when faced with loss, allow yourself time to grieve in the immediate aftermath of the event. Do what needs to be done, but also allow yourself to feel sad. Finally, don't hesitate to reach out for support from others. The strongest people are the first to recognize their needs and know to ask for help.

# PRINCIPLE #92

## Develop coping skills for everyday problems.

Learn to deal with life's little curve balls in order to stand tall when the big pitches are thrown. People who have trouble coping with the setbacks of daily life will have a more difficult time recovering from serious trauma and loss. Start working on your coping skills now so you will be better prepared in case you face a major tragedy. Dealing with small setbacks will help you avoid coming completely unglued when confronted with a true crisis.

# PRINCIPLE #93

## Grief is an individual experience.

There is no formula for grieving, though there are general phases that people go through. In 1969, psychiatrist Elisabeth Kübler-Ross established the 5 stages of grief: denial, anger, bargaining, depression, and acceptance. However, even Kübler-Ross said these were basic guidelines and not strict rules for grieving. In 2004, Kübler-Ross reflected on her stages of grief by saying, "They were never meant to help tuck messy emotions into neat packages. … There is not a typical response to loss, as there is no typical loss. Our grief is as individual as our lives." If your loss or grieving process seems to be unique, remember that grief is as varied as human beings themselves.

# Principle #94

## There is no timetable for grieving.

———————— ✳ ————————

Everyone mourns on their own schedule. For some people the passage of time makes their loss easier. Others find that anniversaries, birthdays, and other milestones are painful reminders that can make their loss feel as if it has just occurred. It may take you some time to navigate through the grief process. Don't berate yourself for not recovering quickly from your tragedy. Doing so will only add guilt on top of pain, increasing your stress. Be gentle with yourself and allow your grieving process to unfold naturally.

# Principle #95

## Let friends and family care for you when you are down.

Everyone needs support at times. When you are feeling sad and find you have trouble coping, let your friends and family know so they can help you. They can do simple things, such as bring you dinner or do a load of laundry. Being with a family member or close friend can remind you who you were before the tragic event occurred. Mourning alone is difficult and can even prolong depression if you lose touch with the outside world. Although you may be in pain, strive to stay connected with others as you cope with your loss.

# Principle #96

## Reminisce about a loved one.

Gather with friends and family and tell stories about the person you've lost. This practice will both honor the person who died and help express your feelings in a healthy way. It is not productive to deny the deceased person's death. Your loved one lives on and will continue to influence and bless your life as you openly share all that he or she meant to you. As the Roman poet Ovid once wrote, "Suppressed grief suffocates, it rages within the breast, and is forced to multiply its strength." So talk about those you miss — they would have wanted it that way.

# PRINCIPLE #97

## Humor can lift the darkest mood.

American humorist Irvin S. Cobb once wrote, "Humor is merely tragedy standing on its head with its pants torn." Without making light of your sadness, find relief by exploring the humorous side of things. If you are down because you have recently been fired, think of funny stories from your work instead of focusing on your lost job. If your sadness stems from the loss of a loved one, think of what would make him or her laugh if he or she were with you. Laughing in the midst of darkness is not disrespectful of sadness but rather shines a light for a brief, necessary moment.

# PRINCIPLE #98

## Know the difference between sadness and depression.

❋

Sadness is a normal response to a loss or tragedy. Sad feelings usually pass after a certain amount of time, but depression includes severe despondency and dejection that is typically felt over a period of time. If you feel unable to cope with your daily activities, avoid friends and family, or are unable to care for yourself, seek professional help. According to the American Psychiatric Association, "Depression is never normal and always produces needless suffering. With proper diagnosis and treatment, the vast majority of people with depression will overcome it."

# Principle #99

## Understand that there are all kinds of reasons to be sad.

Avoid judging another person's reason for feeling sad. The loss of a loved one, divorce, death of a child, or a major illness are experiences most of us would identify as sad. However, sadness generated by the loss of a family heirloom or the foreclosure of a business may not be as easily understandable. Grief is a very personal experience. While sadness can be described in generic terms, the feelings and process required to work through them is unique to each individual. Acknowledging all levels of sadness is important to your relationships. You will likely be rewarded someday for your ability to empathize with a wide range of setbacks.

# Principle #100

## Find a creative outlet to express your feelings.

When you are sad, the last thing you may feel like being is creative. But as the artist Corita Kent said, "Flowers grow from dark moments." When you are sad, try writing a poem or story about the event that troubles you. If you are a visual person, draw or paint using colors that capture your mood. If you are crafty, start a project that will channel your emotional energy in a creative way. Expressing your feelings in a new and creative way will help you cope with sadness.

# Principle #101

## Start new traditions to honor a lost loved one.

Hold on to memories of those who have passed by integrating aspects of their lives into your holidays and traditions. For example, make one of your grandmother's favorite dishes a new staple at the Thanksgiving table. Raise a glass and toast your father on his birthday, telling his favorite story from when you were a child. What was your grandmother's favorite charity? Make a donation in her name every year on her birthday. There are many ways to honor lost loved ones when you find yourself missing them.

# Principle #102

## Sadness is part of
## the human experience.

———————— ❋ ————————

Sociologist Emile Durkheim wrote, "Man could not live if he were entirely impervious to sadness." It is true that sadness is an important part of the natural life cycle. It often takes something tragic to make us realize all that we have to be thankful for. Don't panic if you are feeling down — take a deep breath and remember that you are only human. Understand that this too shall pass and you will be happy again.

# Nurturing Relationships

The relationships you have with your family, friends, and partner are a reflection of who you are. What kinds of people do you surround yourself with? What efforts do you make to enrich your time with these people? Do you treat the people in your life with kindness and respect? The answers to these questions can help determine if your relationships are contributing to your overall happiness.

The relationship you have with yourself is the foundation for all other connections you make with people. If you are miserable and seek to find joy in others, you will be looking for happiness in the wrong place. Know that you are responsible for your own happiness and act accordingly. This will keep you from being codependent, which is an unhealthy approach to all relationships.

In spite of our fast-paced society, make time for meaningful interactions with other people. Dashing off a quick email or leaving a voice mail or text message is no substitute for true interpersonal interaction. In order to live a full and happy life, put time and energy into nurturing your relationships.

Relationship expert Michael Douglas writes, "If your relationship is still important to you, then it will be well worth a little more time and effort. Don't slack off and don't take your partner for granted. Love is like a plant. It needs consistent, careful attention to thrive. Without it, your relationship is destined to wither away." Though Douglas refers specifically to romantic partnerships, his advice can be applied to relationships with your friends and family as well.

Taking the time to carefully tend to your relationships will ensure that they are fulfilling and long-lasting. Studies show that people who have a support network made up of strong relationships recover sooner from illness, live longer, and are generally happier. The following principles show you how to nurture your relationships so you experience the joy that comes from connecting with others.

# Principle #103

## Do not rely on other people for your happiness.

Never enter into a relationship thinking it is going to become the sole source of your happiness. Personal well-being and peace come from an internal source, not an external one. You are responsible for your own happiness. Your happiness is simply not something that others can provide. Relationships should enhance your happiness, not serve as its sole source. Depending on any one person for your happiness will leave you feeling disappointed and unfulfilled.

# PRINCIPLE #104

## Be honest and trustworthy.

— ❊ —

Lies obviously undermine the success of any relationship. Even little white lies can damage your relationships because they chip away at your credibility. As businessman Joseph Sugarman wrote, "Each time you are honest and conduct yourself with honesty, a success force will drive you toward greater success. Each time you lie, even with a little white lie, there are strong forces pushing you toward failure." When you enter into a relationship, you make an unspoken promise to be truthful and trustworthy. Breaking that deal damages both individuals and the relationship.

# Principle #105

## Don't keep score.

Keeping score in a relationship is never productive. Do favors and tasks out of love and responsibility, not to have ammunition for future arguments. Likewise, never do things for others solely so they will someday repay you. As the late Senator Hubert Humphrey once said, "If you keep score on the good things and the bad things, you'll find out that you're a very miserable person. God gave man the ability to forget, which is one of the greatest attributes you have. Because if you remember everything that's happened to you, you generally remember that which is the most unfortunate." To stay happy in your relationships, refrain from keeping score.

# Principle #106

## Keep your commitments.

If you make plans with your friends or family, keep them. Skipping out on a commitment suggests that others are not important to you. If every year your aunt hosts a July Fourth family reunion, put it on your calendar and make sure you attend. When family members look forward to seeing you, and everyone knows the event is a tradition, arrange your schedule ahead of time and be there. Honoring smaller commitments is equally important. Business meetings, lunches with friends, baby showers, and monthly book club meetings are all opportunities to show people you value your relationships.

# Principle #107

## Take responsibility for your words and actions.

Everyone makes mistakes in life, but not everyone takes responsibility for their errors. Accepting responsibility for your words and actions (even when unintentional) is an important part of having successful adult relationships. Humanitarian Werner Erhard wrote, "Being responsible starts with the willingness to deal with a situation from the view of life that you are the generator of what you do, what you have and what you are." So when you misspeak, correct yourself. When you err, recognize it and apologize.

# Principle #108

## Learn to accept apologies.

Accepting an apology is an art that must be mastered to have successful relationships and be happy in life. First, you must let the other person know that their actions or words have hurt you. Hopefully, the person will apologize, which puts the ball back in your court. Do you accept the apology? If you want to continue the relationship, you will have to accept the apology — no matter what was done. The tricky part is letting the apology sink in and heal your relationship. This means you absorb it completely and let the incident go. Accept the eventuality that someday someone will hurt your feelings. You will feel better if you are able to express yourself, accept an apology, and move on.

# Principle #109

## Show appreciation for the people in your life.

Most people remember special days such as birthdays and anniversaries. But you should also select other occasions to show people how much they mean to you. This will greatly enhance your relationships. When shopping, pick up an extra treat for your mom or dad. Plan an unexpected dinner and movie night for your friends. Let your wife come home to love notes left around the house, or devise a plan to go out for no special reason. What you do to express your appreciation is not as important as the thought behind it. Unexpected, thoughtful acts will inject new energy into your relationships and happiness in your life.

# Principle #110

## Honor the relationship you have with yourself.

If you are not good to yourself, why should you expect others to be good to you? Make yourself the most important person in your life. Block out time for yourself and honor that commitment. If something comes up, treat the time you have planned with yourself as any other appointment, and keep it. See a movie, go to dinner, or stay in and take a hot bath. Having a good relationship with yourself is the model for relationships you have with others.

# PRINCIPLE #111

## Set and respect boundaries.

Know what your limits are and stick to them. Likewise, respect the boundaries of others even if you would not choose them yourself. Setting and respecting boundaries is essential in achieving healthy and peaceful relationships. As poet Robert Frost wrote, "Good fences make good neighbors." For example, let people know your house is a "no-call zone" after 7 p.m. if that is when you spend time with your kids. Similarly, make a conscious effort to accommodate the coworker who prefers that others respect his or her personal space. Once you set boundaries, stick to them — switching your limits on and off will breed misunderstandings and confusion.

# Principle #112

## Accept people instead of trying to change them.

One of the greatest things about having relationships with others is that they enhance your life over the years. But over the course of those years, it is likely you will do much learning, growing, and changing. However, just because you changed doesn't mean the people around you have. Remember that qualities that may annoy you now may be the very things that drew you to your friend, partner, or coworker in the first place. Attempts to change people only lead to frustration, so avoid trying to do so.

# Principle #113

## Avoid ultimatums.

※

Ultimatums — threats or unrealistic demands made in the course of an argument — are tools for people who are weak communicators. Ultimatums are similar to childish tantrums, thrown because you do not get what you want from someone. Adults must learn how to disagree without resorting to ultimatums. Nine times out of 10, you will not follow through with your threat anyway, which only reduces your credibility. Find ways to express consequences for certain actions without putting forth an "or else." People naturally fear an ultimatum or they fight it. Neither option is good for your relationship and ultimate happiness.

# Principle #114

## Learn the art of compromise.

— ✳ —

Trust your bond with the people in your life and learn to compromise. For example, when it comes time for your annual family reunion, compromise on the location by meeting someplace in the middle instead of insisting everyone come to you. In arguments, learn to give a little and consider the other person's point of view. Forcing any situation or perspective on another is going to cause them to retreat. Compromising will allow your friends and family to experience the give and take of a partnership and all of you will find your relationships more fulfilling.

# Principle #115

## Don't give in to the green-eyed monster.

———————— ✳ ————————

Jealousy is the great relationship destroyer. Succumbing to jealousy will create distance between you and the people you love. Coveting what your friend has will shrink your capacity to love and support him or her. Jealously guarding your spouse fosters resentment and a tendency toward secrecy. Support the people around you wholeheartedly so that they will want to support you.

# PRINCIPLE #116

## You must love yourself before you love others.

———— ✳ ————

Actress Lucille Ball once said, "Love yourself first and everything else falls into line." Indeed, self-love is directly proportional to the love you feel for others and the love others feel for you. Only enter into a relationship after you are comfortable with yourself. Living on your own, traveling abroad, pursuing an education, and developing your talents are valuable ways to nurture yourself. In many ways, your self-worth and being happy with yourself are the biggest assets that you can bring to your relationships with other people.

# PRINCIPLE #117

## Be someone your partner can lean on.

Consider that between 40 and 50 percent of new marriages will end in divorce. Nobody enters their marriage planning to get divorced, so why are the statistics so high? Too often, what began as a partnership ends up unequal, with one person bearing the brunt of responsibilities. Avoid this by being someone your partner can lean on. If you both work, respect each other's schedules. If your wife is sick, take on extra household duties. When your husband is overly stressed, ask him how you can help. Remember that supporting others is personally rewarding and will bring a new dimension of fulfillment to your life.

# Managing Stress

Studies show that Americans are some of the most stressed people on the planet. According to data from the United Nations, Americans work some of the longest hours of people in any industrialized country. Our demanding schedules naturally lead us to experience high levels of stress, which is detrimental to both our physical and emotional health. Learning how to relax and manage stress is integral to increasing your levels of peace, energy, and happiness.

There are many different ways to implement relaxation techniques into your daily routine. If you have a particularly long day, sneak off and take a power nap for 15 or 20 minutes. A short nap can take the edge off and leave you feeling refreshed. Another strategy for managing stress is to get up a half an hour early and meditate. Meditation rejuvenates your body and settles your mind. Work your way up to meditating twice a day for maximum relaxation results. Learn deep-breathing techniques, and remember to focus on your breathing throughout the day as most of us are shallow breathers, which keeps us tense and irritable. Regular exercise also manages stress and promotes relaxation. Exercise also burns off excess energy and frustration, helps reduce stress-related tension and headaches, and promotes deep sleep at night.

Make time to relax every single day. Taking breaks to breathe and stretch will help you to concentrate and do your best work. According to the Wisconsin Heart and Vascular Clinic, "Therapeutic relaxation techniques help teach the mind to slow down and focus on breathing in order to reconnect with the body. The purpose is to bring our bodies back to a state of equilibrium, or balance, following disruptions that put stress on all the systems the body regulates." With practice, relaxation becomes an indispensable part of your day. You will feel refreshed and rested, and your mood will improve, as you master relaxation. The following principles will help you learn how to relax and manage stress in order to become a much happier person.

# Principle #118

## Learn to say "no."

Having too many plans in a week is sure to stress anyone out. Therefore it is important to say "no" to nonessential social events. Though it is nice to be invited to things, it is not necessary to accept every invitation. Saying "no" will not only reduce stress but also keep you healthy. According to the Centers for Disease Control, the leading 6 causes of death in the U.S. — heart disease, cancer, lung ailments, accidents, cirrhosis of the liver, and suicide — are all brought on at least in part by stress. Feel empowered to practice saying "no" when it is appropriate and in your best interest. Love yourself enough to set limits on what can be demanded of you.

# Principle #119

## Keep your home and office organized.

Being organized reduces the stress that comes from not knowing where to find something in a pinch. Clutter takes up physical space and negatively affects your mental health and happiness. So put the dishes away after you wash them. Fold and put away laundry. Hang up your coat when you take it off. Clear off your desk at the end of the day. And be sure to have a pen and paper handy near the phone. When you're finished with something, always put it back where it belongs. Keeping your surroundings in order will help you live a stress-free life and promote a stronger feeling of happiness.

# Principle #120

## Make time for yourself to do absolutely nothing.

Turn the ringer off on your phone. Shut off the television, stereo, and computer. Sit in your favorite comfortable spot and listen to the quiet. Slow down your breathing and take a deep breath if needed. Ask your family to leave you alone for 20 minutes each evening as you wind down and refresh your system. Journalist Sydney J. Harris reminds us that even though it may seem impossible to do so, the most important time to relax is when you feel you cannot afford to do it.

# PRINCIPLE #121

## Take a break.

— ❋ —

Stress is a widespread problem in a world where everyone is constantly "plugged in." People spend their waking hours tied to email, BlackBerries, cell phones, computers, and other instruments that keep them on the go. If this is your lifestyle, be sure to make time to unplug. Just 20 minutes spent taking a quick nap or a relaxing walk dissolves layers of pent-up stress. In addition to feeling better and happier, you will be helping your employer. According to the Centers for Disease Control, U.S. employers spend $300 billion, or $7,500 per employee, each year on stress-related issues, including reduced productivity, absenteeism, health insurance costs, and employee turnover.

# Principle #122

## Learn to daydream.

Let your mind wander. In your imagination, go to a place that makes you feel relaxed and happy. Imagine drifting in a canoe down a winding river. Maybe you would prefer to lie on a beach in the Caribbean. No matter where your mind takes you, let it drift and rest there for a little while each day. When you come back, write down what you thought of and how it made you feel. Refer to this daydream book when you're feeling stressed — it will help you remember the benefits of daydreaming, and perhaps someday those dreams will be realized.

# PRINCIPLE #123

## Laugh out loud often.

─────────────── ✳ ───────────────

Studies show that laughter reduces stress, lowers blood pressure, elevates mood, and boosts the immune system. Laughter also improves brain functioning, increases oxygen in the blood, fosters connection with others, and makes you feel good all over. Children in nursery school laugh approximately 300 times a day, while adults laugh, at most, only 17 times per day. So why should children reap all the benefits? Incorporate a good chuckle into your day to reduce stress and promote relaxation and happiness.

# Principle #124

## Slow it down a notch.

When you rush through meals, conversations, and experiences, you end up rushing through life. Slow down and chew your food. Taste it. Relish it. Enjoy the person you are speaking with — actually listen to his or her comments without thinking of what you will say next. Drive the speed limit and let someone into your lane ahead of you. Taking your time can prevent stressful accidents and misunderstandings. Finally, indulge in the joy of taking your time in order to experience the unexpected. As author Douglas Pagels writes, "Some of the secret joys of living are not found by rushing from point A to point B, but by inventing some imaginary letters along the way."

# Principle #125

## Treat yourself to a massage.

— ❋ —

Treat yourself to relaxing indulgences such as a massage. Massage therapy helps to relieve tension headaches, eye strain, muscle tension, and stiffness. A massage can cost between $55 and $125, but how many times have we spent more than that in a store and still come home feeling sad or lonely? Massages do not have to be expensive. Many massage schools offer discounted services so their students can practice their skills. Or, ask a friend or partner to exchange massages. If massages are not your thing, try indulging in another relaxing activity to reduce stress, such as a daytime nap or a long, hot bath.

# Principle #126

## Find a hobby that relaxes you and indulge in it.

Make time each week for a hobby that you find relaxing. For instance, take a pottery or painting class — you will likely find it satisfying to produce something beautiful with your own hands that you can be proud of. Hobbies have been medically proven to reduce stress and increase happiness. One study published in the Journal of the American Medical Association, of 30 female heart patients, reported significant decreases in heart rate and blood pressure while subjects worked on a simple craft project. Improved health is just one example of the many positive benefits a hobby can bring to your life.

# Principle #127

## Exercise to reduce stress.

It is true that exercise is an excellent stress-reduction tool for several reasons. Exercise helps release built-up tension and helps you relax. Exercise also releases endorphins in the brain, promoting feelings of happiness and well-being. Some forms of exercise involve social interaction, which can also be great for stress reduction. The benefits of exercise — such as a toned body and weight loss — can also increase your self-esteem. So make sure to incorporate some form of physical activity into your daily routine.

# Principle #128

## Live within your means.

According to the American Psychological Association, 73 percent of Americans list money as the number one factor that affects their stress level. Therefore, to reduce stress strive to live within your means. Establish a budget and stick to it. If you cannot afford to purchase something nonessential with cash, don't buy it. You may not have the fleeting instant gratification that a fancy skirt or new CD may bring, but you will achieve the peace of mind that comes with avoiding debt and living responsibly.

# PRINCIPLE #129

## Exhale your tension.

Shallow breathing prevents relaxation and causes tension to stay deep within your muscles. Breathing deeply before making an important decision can help clear your mind and prevent making an impulsive choice. Practice proper breathing by inhaling deeply for at least 5 seconds. Exhale slowly, counting back from 5 to 1. Repeat 5 or 6 times at least several times a day to maximize relaxation.

# Principle #130

## Don't be a workaholic.

Writer Margaret Fuller once noted, "Men for the sake of getting a living forget to live." If you find yourself devoting inordinate chunks of time to work, ask yourself, what are you getting out of it? Refrain from working more than 9 hours a day, and take at least 1 day a week to not work at all. Instead of working yourself to the point of exhaustion every day, make sure the hours you spend at work are quality ones. The world is not likely to fall apart if you do not check your email or return a phone call immediately, so it makes no sense to add such stress to your life.

# Overcoming Fear

Our fears are some of the biggest obstacles to happiness. We learn how and what to fear as we grow up. Of course, fear is natural and necessary in certain instances. Fear activates our fight-or-flight response — the response that will get us out of a burning building or allow us to fight off an attacker. But when fear prevents us from living a full and happy life, it must be brought under control.

Unchecked fear can turn into a serious condition known as panic disorder. According to Dr. Edmund J. Bourne, fear-based disorders such as panic attacks, anxiety, and phobias have reached epidemic proportions. Bourne blames the increase of these disorders on "an outcome of cumulative stress acting over time." People with uncontrollable anxiety about being around crowds or about making some kind of social blunder can become so fearful that they rarely leave their homes, resulting in social isolation. Getting your fear under control is necessary to prevent more serious conditions from developing. If you think you may already have a fear-based disorder, it is important to seek professional help as soon as possible.

Some fears are the result of early negative experiences. What may have begun as a simple dislike or discomfort due to unfamiliarity can worsen over time, causing terror and dread. For instance, if as a child you hurt yourself riding an escalator, being afraid of escalators would be a natural response. However, if you continue avoiding them as you grow up, that fear could develop into panic when faced with the need to use an escalator.

A person cannot find happiness if his or her life is lived in constant fear. The principles in the following chapter will teach you how to overcome and manage your fears. The first thing to learn is to face your fear — no matter how big or small. Much of the work it takes to overcome fear has to do with your perception of what is happening. Use the following principles to change the way you think and to push fear out and make room for happiness.

# Principle #131

## Educate yourself about your fears.

It is likely that your fears have no basis in reality. Should you be concerned that the airplane you're on is going to crash? According to the National Transportation Safety Board, the odds of being killed in a plane crash are 52.6 million to 1. The best way to confront your fears is to educate yourself. Make a list of your fears and research them. Write a fear on one side of an index card and the reality on the other side. Carry these cards with you and refer to them until you are firmly grounded in what is likely to occur rather than what you are afraid will occur.

# Principle #132

## Use affirmations to feel safe.

Without realizing it, we use our minds to reinforce our fears. So much time is spent telling ourselves "I can't do this" or "I won't be able to cope" that we build up fear instead of tearing it down. Instead, replace negative thoughts with positive ones to dissolve fear. Inspirational author Louise Hay recommends the following affirmation to combat anxiety: "I love and approve of myself and I trust in the process of life. I am safe." Repeating this or a similar affirmation frequently will help you find inner calm, build your self-esteem, and teach your mind to handle whatever life throws at you.

# Principle #133

## Visualize your fear as a tangible object, then reshape it.

There are many ways to visualize whatever you fear as an object under your control. Imagine your fear of public speaking as a giant mound of sand. If you allow your imagination to run wild it could become quicksand and threaten to drown you. Instead, take control of your thoughts and turn that mound of sand into a castle. You determine its shape, size, and features. Use visualization to change your fear from a terrifying possibility to an incredible opportunity and tackle something you've never had the courage to attempt before.

# Principle #134

## Use relaxation techniques.

Combat fear by practicing relaxation techniques every day for at least 20 to 30 minutes. The goal is to put yourself in a relaxed and fearless state. Achieving a relaxed state takes work. Deep breathing is a particularly effective relaxation technique. To get the most out of deep breathing, place your right hand on your chest and your left hand on your stomach. When you are deep breathing properly, your left hand should move up and down, but your right hand should stay still. Other relaxation techniques include meditation, yoga, listening to soothing music or fountains, visualizing a peaceful scene, and achieving muscle relaxation. Each of these will calm you, causing you to be less prone to fear.

# Principle #135

## Confront your fears.

Writer Henry S. Haskins thought of fear in the following way: "Panic at the thought of doing a thing is a challenge to do it." Turn your greatest fear on its head by confronting it. If you feel crowded in public places (as do 1 in 5 Americans, according to the National Institute of Mental Health), purposely seek out a crowd and become part of it. If you fear the dentist (as do 58 percent of Americans), schedule an appointment with your dentist to have him or her explain what goes on during a check-up. Confronting your fears will demystify them, allowing them to be conquered.

# PRINCIPLE #136

## Do not try to control life.

The sooner you accept that life is not controllable, the quicker you will be released from many of your fears. Fear is often the distress felt at being unable to control your environment. The truth is that much of life is out of your hands, and that's nothing to be afraid of. Get a handle on life, not by trying to control it but by learning as much as you can about the things in life that you fear. As scientist Marie Curie said, "Nothing in life is to be feared. It is only to be understood."

# Principle #137

## Identify fears and let them go.

If fear is running your life, sit down and make a list of what actually scares you and why. Start with the biggest and work your way down. Let's say fear of failure is first on your list. Write it down, and then under it write how many times you've actually failed at something. If the list is long, then cross each past event off the list and let it stay in the past. If your list is short or you cannot come up with any major failures, then realize your fear is unfounded and let it go.

# Principle #138

## Make a plan of action.

Make a daily plan of action to conquer fears. Your list should include: 1) Getting 20 to 30 minutes of daily exercise — this will help you burn off nervous energy. 2) Exchanging negative self-talk with "can do" statements, which will help replace your fear with confidence, and 3) Changing behaviors that you practice when you're afraid — if you pace when nervous, try taking 10 deep breaths instead. Tailor your list to your specific fears and be sure to stick to it. Taking action is the first step to feeling better and happier.

# Principle #139

## Let things unfold naturally.

You can't always know how things will turn out. Find a way to be okay with that. Learn to relax and let events unfold naturally instead of trying to control the outcome. If you obsess over what comes next, you will miss what is happening right now. Part of the fun of life is the surprises that pop up now and then. Author Andre Gide once wrote, "There are very few monsters who warrant the fear we have of them." Don't let your fears control you and cause you to miss life's many pleasures.

# PRINCIPLE #140

## Seek professional help when fear becomes unmanageable.

— ✻ —

Do your fears prevent you from living a normal life? If so, you may be part of the 10 percent of Americans who suffer from one or more specific phobias, or part of the 2 percent who suffer from panic disorder, according to mental health professionals. If you suspect you have a fear-based disorder, get professional help. Therapy and medication can bring your anxiety down to a manageable level. There is no shame in recognizing when a problem becomes too big for you to handle alone.

# Developing a Sense of Purpose

It is physically and emotionally healthy to develop a strong sense of purpose. The state of mind you have when absorbed in accomplishing a goal is an engaged, satisfied state. Those who have learned to develop a sense of purpose are the most likely to be happy and healthy.

As adults we tend to let our hopes and dreams fall by the wayside. But hopes and dreams can be the foundation for many attainable goals. Let your mind wander and see where it leads you. Write down when you feel particularly inspired by an idea for the future. According to Utah State University Human Development Specialist Tom Lee, "As youth grow to adulthood, they should develop a sense of purpose about their lives, cultivate dreams and aspirations, then make daily choices which lead to those dreams."

Finding your purpose can be a daunting task, but it is possible.

What are your strengths and talents? As children, each of us show an affinity for something — did you excel at art or music? These are talents and skills that can be factored in when defining your overall direction in life.

Setting small, attainable goals and working toward each of them in turn will help you achieve your ultimate purpose. For example, if your ultimate goal is to open your own restaurant, make a list of the steps to achieve this goal. On this list should be saving money for start-up fees, consulting with a lender, drafting a business plan, visiting restaurants to see how they operate, and coming up with ways to market your establishment. The choices you make each day should always move you toward your goal. Work or volunteer at a restaurant to learn how it operates. Take a class on business management and marketing. Educating yourself on how to realize your dream will help you define your goal more clearly.

Give your life direction by chipping away at a list of things you want to accomplish. Use the following principles to develop something you want to work toward; it will improve your self-esteem and contribute to your overall sense of happiness.

# Principle #141

## Let your dreams open up possibilities.

Henry David Thoreau once wrote, "If you have built castles in the air, your work need not be lost; that is where they should be. Now put the foundations under them." In this spirit, allow your dreams to form the basis of your goals. Start by revisiting the dreams of your childhood and take an inventory of the ones you have accomplished. Which dreams remain? Do you dare strive for them now? Let's say you imagined yourself sitting on a porch swing, sipping lemonade. Eventually, this may become, "I hope to own a country home." Make this both a dream and a goal to work toward.

# Principle #142

## Create a list of short-term goals.

To jump-start a newfound feeling of accomplishment, create a list of short-term goals. These can be things you can complete on a daily or weekly basis. Some can be errands that need to be done, such as getting your oil changed, picking up dry cleaning, or going grocery shopping. Others can be activities you've been meaning to do but haven't gotten around to in a while, such as reading a good book, organizing your photos into albums, or cleaning out the garage. Cross items off your list as you do them. This will give you an immediate sense of accomplishment and keep you motivated to work on your larger goals.

# Principle #143

## Create a list of long-term goals.

Consider what your long-term goals might be. Do you want to get an advanced degree? Start a business? Have a family? Or own a home? Write down your long-term goals and put them in a highly visible place so that you can revisit them often. Reviewing this list of goals often will remind you of the things that are important to you. In turn, this will make you work on the things that will help you achieve those goals. If you do not know where you are going, you will never get there. Likewise, if you do not know what you want to achieve in life, you will never achieve anything that is important to you.

# Principle #144

## Recognize your achievements.

Although some of your life goals may not yet be accomplished, it is likely you already have many achievements already under your belt. Relive your successes. Pore over them and let them sink in. Realize that what you have done up to this point counts and is an important part of your life's direction. Furthermore, realizing what you have already accomplished can lead you to brainstorm about new goals. For example, perhaps a few years ago you joined a book club. This accomplishment might in turn lead you to realize you'd like to get a master's degree in English, or open a book store, or write short stories. Build on your successes and climb higher, using them as a strong foundation.

# Principle #145

## Make your daily activities an investment in your life bank.

———————— ✳ ————————

Having no sense of purpose is extremely frustrating and demoralizing. You get up and go to work every day, but you don't know what you're working toward. You operate on routine and memory. You may even catch yourself accidentally driving to work on a Saturday morning. Wake up and pay attention to your life! Imagine that every thought and action is currency, and your life is your savings account. Each step you take toward fulfilling your purpose and improving your happiness is money in the bank.

# Principle #146

## Live a life of purpose.

———————— ✳ ————————

Richard Leider, author of *The Power of Purpose*, wrote, "The purpose of life is to live a life of purpose." Developing your purpose is a process and there are several tools you can use to advance your goals. Use introspection to reveal what your goals are. Next, discuss your goals with someone else. This can help crystallize what you want to accomplish. Finally, reflect on what you have done so far that contributes to your goals. If you practice these steps with regularity, you *are* living your purpose, and your goals are within reach. Nothing can compare to the feeling of satisfaction that comes from reaching a goal that originated in your own heart and mind.

# Principle #147

## Do at least one thing every day that brings you closer to your goals.

Make time every day to do one small thing that contributes to your long-term goals. If you want to run a marathon some day, start exercising. Walk at first, increasing the distance and intensity until you are running. Running each day is good for your body and mind, but running for a purpose makes it more fulfilling. Every extra mile you run brings you closer to your ultimate goal of running a marathon. All long-term goals can be broken up into smaller activities you can work on from the first day that you set out to achieve them. If the final destination seems too far, just start with the first step.

# PRINCIPLE #148

## Get back in tune with your childhood inclinations.

T.S. Eliot once wrote, "Time you enjoyed wasting is not wasted time." Revisit the talents and interests you had as a child. They are often great indicators for how you can be most fulfilled. Adults believe they must outgrow certain childhood pursuits, but remembering what you used to enjoy can often point to your hidden purpose. For example, if you used to love riding your bike after school, perhaps you should purchase a bike and ride it to work. Combining childhood joy with adult sensibility is a great way to realize your purpose.

# Principle #149

## Try new things until something clicks.

Go outside your safety zone to open yourself to new endeavors. For example, if you are a computer person, try a creative writing class; if you have never been athletic, join a gym. Pushing the boundaries of your life can open new doors. During any one of these new endeavors, you will likely meet people who will unexpectedly influence you. Live your life as if there is something to be discovered with every decision. You will later be surprised at how seemingly random decisions helped shape your purpose. As Robert Louis Stevenson wrote, "The mark of a good action is that it appears inevitable in retrospect." Be proud and find happiness in trying new things.

# Principle #150

Explore your spirituality and investigate a faith that appeals to you.

---- ✳ ----

Finding your purpose ties in with whether you connect to a higher power. Spirituality is grounding and affirming because it offers rules that can help dictate the direction your life takes. Following religious traditions also connects you to a group that is acting on the same principles, working toward a common purpose. Finally, feeling connected to God and to the service of your religion will provide shelter in the storms of life.

# Principle #151

## Experience new things.

———————— ✳ ————————

Even if you are not sure where you are going, stay in motion. Do something outside your normal routine every day. Take a different route to work. Try a new coffee shop. Introduce yourself to a neighbor. Sticking to your same routine day in and day out provides no opportunities for new experiences. When you look at the ground while you walk, you miss the sights, sounds, and signs all around you. Treat everything you do as an opportunity to learn something new that may help inform your life and purpose. As Mother Teresa once said, "Life is a promise; fulfill it."

# Principle #152

## Give yourself to a cause you care about.

There are many reasons to give your time and energy to a cause you care about, and one of them is to sharpen your sense of purpose. Studies show that people who devote at least 1 to 2 hours per week to a worthy cause feel an immediate boost in their self-confidence, self-worth, and sense of purpose. People who volunteer for Habitat for Humanity, for instance, report feeling satisfied when their work results in a home for a low-income family. It is no wonder, then, that helping others is often cited as the single most influential factor in finding one's purpose.

# PRINCIPLE #153

## Research how to make your dream a reality.

Whatever your dream, there is a way to make it real. Write down your dream on a large piece of paper, or paint the words on a canvas, and hang it in your home. Next, record the steps you need to take to reach your dream. If you want to live on a sailboat, you will need to save money, learn about boats, and learn how to sail. Each major step may have many little steps, so you may be working toward your dream for a long time — possibly your entire life. The good news is you will have found your purpose.

# Increasing Your Self-Esteem

According to *Consumer Reports*, the average American is exposed to 247 commercial messages every day. Products sell by creating a need. To make us believe that we need something, we are told repeatedly that something very important is missing from our lives. These messages make us realize what we don't have and then we feel dissatisfied. These messages range from "you need to lose weight" to "your car is worthless." Combating these messages can be challenging. But if you improve how you regard yourself by improving your self-image, you will be able to sort through outside voices that tell you that you don't have enough without letting them affect your outlook and happiness.

Your upbringing certainly influences how you register an advertising assault. As a child were you praised, listened to, and treated with respect and trust? Or were you criticized, ignored, or expected to be perfect? People who were raised to have high self-esteem may not be as susceptible to advertising as children who had less support. However, no adult is immune to such hits to their self-confidence.

The best way to boost your self-esteem is to use the most powerful tool you have — your thoughts. Every negative thing you tell yourself throughout the day (*I'm too fat, I'm ugly, My nose is too big, I am not smart enough*) can be cancelled out with a positive message. Positive self-talk leads to a positive self-image. Insulate yourself from the forces that want to tear down your confidence by arming yourself with a strong layer of self-esteem. Author Louise Hart wrote, "Self-esteem is as important to our well-being as legs are to a table. It is essential for physical and mental health and for happiness."

The following principles will teach you how to increase your self-esteem. They will show you how to make the decision to be kind to yourself instead of overly critical. Unbridled self-criticism does not benefit you in any way. In fact, it stands directly in your way of experiencing the joys self-confidence affords. These and other insights are found in the following chapter; use them to boost your self-esteem and realize true happiness.

# Principle #154

## Believe you have tried your best.

You may not be excellent at everything you do, but you certainly can try your best. Knowing that you have given 100 percent has to be enough sometimes. If you have never ice skated before, you can't expect to be performing spins your first time on the ice. So, acknowledge your limitations and move on. Now, focus on your strengths — you tried something new and made it around the rink twice! Feel good about yourself by paying attention to what you do well.

# Principle #155

## Silence your inner critic.

The first step to becoming immune to the criticisms of others is to silence the critic within yourself. As an African proverb states, "When there is no enemy within, the enemies outside cannot hurt you." Counteract nasty self-talk with reassuring, productive thoughts. Remind yourself of specific times when you did something well. Keep track of your accomplishments to banish self-criticism. Remember that everything is relative; what you make of your accomplishments is what matters. You can be happy you were able to go around the rink twice, or you can be unhappy because you were *only* able to go around the rink twice. The choice is yours.

# PRINCIPLE #156

## Take care of yourself.

If you don't feel physically well, it will be difficult to feel emotionally well. Even when stretched thin, make sure to practice basic self-care. Get outdoors every day for at least 30 minutes. The fresh air and exercise will clear your head and release endorphins, which will give you a natural high. Make healthy choices when you eat. Eating foods that nourish your body (greens, lean protein, whole grains) will give you energy to carry you through your day. Building self-care into your daily routine boosts your confidence and with regular practice will elevate your mood, thereby increasing your happiness.

# PRINCIPLE #157

## Love your body — it's the only one you've got.

If you don't like your physique, you are not alone. A poll taken by *Psychology Today* revealed that 24 percent of women and 17 percent of men said they would shave 3 years off their lives to become thinner. A combined assault against your body image is launched daily by the advertising industry. When you read a magazine or watch TV, keep in mind that advertising exists to create a need. Few of us are equipped to combat these messages, but one tool you do have is your self-esteem. Build it up by telling yourself you are perfect as you are, and don't compare yourself to unrealistic images from TV and magazines.

# Principle #158

## Keep a running list of your accomplishments.

It is crucial to your self-worth and overall happiness to recognize and celebrate your accomplishments. Make a list and in bold marker at the top write, "Accomplishments." Each time you do something you are proud of write it down. Do not downplay that you received a great review at work, saved $50 by shopping with coupons, made someone laugh, or were able to fix the toaster — put it all on the list. These are great accomplishments. Hang the list where you will see it several times a day. Nothing makes you feel like an accomplished person more than that you completed what you set out to do.

# Principle #159

## Forgive yourself for not being who you thought you'd be by now.

It is often said, "To wish you were someone else is to waste the person you are." Life may not be what you thought it was going to be, but don't let that get you down. Instead of focusing on what you are not, focus on what you are. Note things you like about your job. Be thankful for friendships. Celebrate your partner and family. If you are single, relish your independence. You can always think of not-so-great things about yourself. The key to happiness is to concentrate on the great ones.

# Principle #160

## Reward your successes.

Many of us have no problem berating ourselves when we mess up, yet we often let our successes go unnoticed. This kind of imbalance is sure to diminish self-worth over time. So, even the scales by rewarding your successes, no matter how small. Figuring out how to put together a new bookshelf on your own is a victory. Treat it as such! Place your favorite books on the shelves, then sit quietly and appreciate your achievement. Noticing and celebrating your successes on a regular basis is important for maintaining a balanced self-image. Nothing encourages you to work harder at achieving future goals as recognizing ones you have already met.

# Principle #161

## Face your fears.

It is true that most often the only thing to be feared is fear itself. In many cases, fear is a direct result of low self-esteem. To reduce fear and increase self-esteem, you must face your fears, conquer them, and move past them. Normalize feelings of anxiety by telling yourself, "This is okay, I am okay." Remind yourself that most fear is actually being afraid to feel afraid. Become immersed in what you are doing. Each time you do this your fear will become less pronounced and your confidence will increase.

# Principle #162

## Use positive self-talk.

*Saturday Night Live* character Stuart Smalley used to close his sketch with, "I am good enough, I am smart enough, and gosh darn it, people like me." Though this was meant to be funny, the remark is rooted in truth. You probably spend time each day telling yourself what you should have done, what you could have done better, or what you find unsatisfying about yourself. These messages will stall your happiness and prevent your self-confidence from blossoming. To nurture your whole being, change the way you talk to yourself. Within a few weeks of using positive self-talk you will notice you feel much better and happier about yourself.

# PRINCIPLE #163

## Try new things.

One of the best ways to improve your self-esteem is to try new things. You may not always succeed in everything, but by seeking new experiences and facing new challenges you will develop a wide range of skills, talents, and qualities. More important, you will demystify failure. Realize that being occasionally wrong or not the best at something is not the end of the world. As writer Peter T. McIntyre once observed, "Confidence comes not from always being right but from not fearing to be wrong."

# Principle #164

## Don't give people permission to make you feel inferior.

Everyone receives a hurtful comment now and then, but only you determine whether or not the barb gets under your skin. As comedian W.C. Fields once said, "It ain't what they call you, it's what you answer to." Raise yourself above the petty insults and criticisms of others. Know that you are better than those whose only way to elevate themselves is to put others down.

# PRINCIPLE #165

## Understand that people don't look at your imperfections.

Those of us with the lowest self-esteem often tend to imagine that people are constantly focusing on us. As author Olin Miller once famously quipped, "We probably wouldn't worry about what people think of us if we could know how seldom they do." Take comfort in knowing that people don't notice all the little things about yourself that you do. This is easy to see when you realize that you don't notice the little imperfections in the people around you. The only person that notices that little blemish on your face or that you gained 5 pounds is you.

# CREATING A HAPPY ENVIRONMENT

We tend to overlook how our environment impacts us. But our surroundings influence our mood and inspire us, for better or worse. Creating an environment that facilitates happiness is a key component to becoming a happier person.

According to researchers with *TV Turnoff Week*, the average American household has the television on for 7 hours and 40 minutes each day. That means the television is on more than 50 hours per week! An environment in which there is constant noise and distraction is not a place that will facilitate relaxation or happiness. Turning off the television is one step toward making your home a comfortable, happy, and stress-free zone.

Consider how much noise your ears must filter every day. The beeping of trucks backing up, lawn mowers, loud radios, bus brakes — you probably don't even realize how this constant noise negatively affects your quality of life. According to the Noise Pollution Clearinghouse, "Noise negatively affects human health and well-being. Problems related to noise include hearing loss, stress, high blood pressure, sleep loss, distraction and lost productivity, and a general reduction in the quality of life and opportunities for tranquility." Making your primary environment a quiet place will give your senses a much-needed rest.

To add more tranquility to your home, accessorize with scented candles and have them ready to light when the mood strikes. Aromatherapy oils can be used in the bath or in special burners to add pleasing scents to every room. Adding plants to your home not only brightens your space, but also detoxifies the air you breathe by adding oxygen. If you are able, consider owning a pet. Studies show that having a pet reduces stress-related medical issues and alleviates loneliness.

Sit down in a quiet room, close your eyes, and imagine a peaceful home. What does it look like? What does it smell like? Once you imagine a serene home environment, take a look around and make some changes. Time in your home should bring you pleasure, not frustration. The following principles will help you create an environment that facilitates happiness.

# PRINCIPLE #166

## Incorporate the practice of Feng Shui in your home.

Feng Shui expert Jayme Barrett suggests you ask yourself 4 questions when trying to decide whether to keep an object in your home: Do I need it? Do I love it? Does it make me happy? If you answer "no" to all of these questions, get rid of it. Your living space is a mirror of who you are. According to the ancient Chinese practice of Feng Shui, the choices you make when decorating affect your quality of life. The right choices can add vitality, while wrong choices (like dark colors and heavy curtains) may weigh you down and anchor your mood.

# PRINCIPLE #167

## Clean and remove the clutter from your home.

Instead of letting your mood be negatively affected by your disorganized house, take action and get things in order. Cleaning will take less time if you replace things after you use them as you go about your day. When you're finished with the iron, put it away. Hang up your towel after you shower. Put your clothes away after you do laundry. Do the dishes each night to wake up to a clean and ready kitchen. Taking care of simple things as they come up will alleviate the frustration of a cluttered home. Beginning your day in a clean house is sometimes all it takes to start out on the right foot.

# Principle #168

## Allow sunshine to enter your surroundings.

Open your windows and doors and let the sunshine in. Fresh air and light will do wonders for elevating your mood. Bright sunshine will lighten even the darkest corners. Clean air drifting through your home creates a relaxing, invigorating environment. Author Zane Madison writes, "A good breath of fresh air can revitalize, energize, and stimulate the mind that has been dulled, as well as the body that is fatigued." Air and sunshine are readily available, so use them often to improve your day. You will start to look forward to your "open window" time and enjoy the home you've created.

# Principle #169

## Use aromatherapy to elevate your mood.

Studies show that use of essential oils boosts immunity, aids with digestion, improves circulation and respiratory functioning, relaxes the muscles, and calms the mind. Using just a few drops of lavender, geranium, bergamot, chamomile, or cypress in a warm bath can help you to relax at the end of a stressful day. For a pick-me-up, take a shower, bathe, or use lotion infused with lime, lemon, orange, or grapefruit oil. Inhale a citrus scent as you apply it to your skin and feel it awaken your senses. Notice and enjoy your experience. Essential oils can also be heated to disperse pleasing scents throughout your home.

# Principle #170

## Green your environment.

Adding indoor plants to your home has many benefits. Plants absorb carbon dioxide and release oxygen. Plants also metabolize a host of toxins in your home, helping to purify the air you breathe. Studies have shown that plants remove toxins such as formaldehyde and benzene from the air. In addition, caring for plants aids relaxation. Harry Coverts of *Gardner's Path* writes, "Plants help you relax. I'm not talking about the joys of gardening. I'm talking about sitting back and looking at a plant you are helping to grow, admiring its simple complexity and noticing the slow changes it goes through." Plants are an inexpensive and easy way to add vitality to your personal space.

# PRINCIPLE #171

## Get a pet, stress less.

Countless studies show that having a pet is good for your health and happiness. Pets improve your overall mood. Just try not to smile when you are greeted by a loving dog whose entire life revolves around you, even after fighting traffic for an hour. A recent study showed that stockbrokers in New York who had dogs or cats as pets had lower blood pressure than those who did not. Pets reduce anxiety and stress; dogs, in particular, force you to get out and exercise. Finally, adding a pet to your home ensures that you will always have company.

# Principle #172

## Limit your exposure to the news.

Most people watch or listen to the news as they dress for the day or drive to work. But often, the top stories in the United States include murder, war, terrorism, and natural disasters. Did you need to know this information to function throughout your day? While it is important to stay in touch with the world's events, choose a time less critical to your mood than the morning to fill yourself in on the news. Try starting your day with music instead. You will likely feel lighter and less stressed out.

# Principle #173

## Surround yourself with good memories.

Decorate your living space with things that mean something to you. Whenever you travel, pick up a piece that can be displayed somewhere that will remind you of your adventure. Put up photographs of friends and family so your home is infused with their presence. Prominently display diplomas, certificates, or other markers of success that make you proud. Filling your home with warm memories makes it a space in which you want to spend your time.

# Principle #174

## Use candles to set the tone.

To relax in the evening, light a vanilla pillar candle and settle down to watch it flicker. Having a party? Fill white paper bags with sand, then place tea lights inside them to light the walkway. Taper candles can set a romantic mood for when you want to connect with your partner. Relax with a warm bath in a candlelit bathroom. This sort of illumination is an inexpensive way to set the tone for any occasion. Furthermore, lighting candles around the home will give your eyes a break from the strain caused by the computer screen and harsh artificial lights.

# Principle #175

## Make your home a noise-free zone.

If you are one of 80 percent of Americans who live in urban or suburban places, you are constantly bombarded with noise. Every day we hear car horns, garbage trucks, airplanes, landscaping equipment, cell phones, radios, televisions, and appliances. Constant noise has been proven to increase irritation and stress levels. To the best of your ability, for a few hours each day, make your home a noise-free zone. Turn off the TV, stereo, and ringer on your phone. Tell your kids it is "quiet time" and encourage them to read or play in their rooms. Use daily quiet time to decompress and soothe frazzled nerves.

# TAKING TIME FOR YOURSELF

There are 24 hours in a day, and yet most of us claim it is impossible to set aside one of those hours for ourselves. When life gets hectic and stressful, don't cast aside your own needs. Taking time for yourself each day is necessary to decompress and prevent burnout. If you are stretched thin and feeling tense, your job performance will suffer as will your relationships.

You may equate setting aside time for yourself every day with selfishness. This is a myth that author Julia Cameron debunks: "Every time you commit to some self-nurturing project, there's the voice of your conditioning that raises its head and says, 'Oh dear aren't you being selfish.' We lose ourselves because we are afraid of being selfish, but when we turn around and take care of ourselves, we actually become much happier and generous people."

The surest way to claim time for yourself is to schedule it and honor those appointments. According to the Palo Alto Medical Foundation, "People who plan their time tend to be happier than people who wander through life being bored or not knowing what they want to do." Plan activities that you enjoy. Try something new each week — a new exercise class, maybe, or a hot rock massage. Most likely, you will have to defend this appointment to others who try and convince you to reschedule your massage or workout for another time. That is when you need to be firm about your needs. Time with yourself is every bit as important (and sometimes even more so) as the time you give to others. If you don't take care of yourself first you won't be able to care for others.

Honoring the appointments you make with yourself will increase your self-esteem because you are telling yourself "my time and mental health are important to me." After a few weeks of practice, your scheduled "me time" will become an indispensable part of your overall well-being. The following principles offer suggestions on how to maximize the art of taking time for yourself.

# Principle #176

## Claim alone time for at least an hour every day.

Spend at least 1 hour a day by yourself. This can be time spent doing anything you'd like, as long as it contributes to your overall well-being. Tailor your daily self-hour to your particular interests and needs. If you need to relax, focus on activities that involve deep breathing, like yoga. If you need to boost your activity level, go for a brisk walk. The key to the "hour of you" is to nurture yourself in any way you like or need.

# Principle #177

## Read a book.

Make a list of books that you have always wanted to read. Set aside at least 15 minutes per day to spend with your favorite book. You'll be surprised how quickly you check books off your list if you stick to the 15-minute rule. Reading before bed relaxes you, and reading a wide variety of materials increases vocabulary and comprehension, which gives you the added benefit of expanding self-confidence.

# PRINCIPLE #178

## Take a hike.

———————— ❋ ————————

Getting out in nature is good for the body and mind. Go for a walk or hike at least once a week. The natural environment will help you to clear your head. According to a report by John Davis, PhD, breaking up the monotony of your normal environment by spending time in nature can help reduce burnout. Frequent visits to a park or other outdoor scenic setting reduce stress levels by removing the distractions caused by modern technology. Completing a difficult hike or overcoming some other obstacle presented in the wilderness has a positive impact on self-esteem. So treat yourself to a dose of nature therapy.

# PRINCIPLE #179

## Organize your photos.

— ✳ —

Whether it takes one night or several days, spend time with yourself and your past by organizing your photos. Start by collecting stray photos from every corner of your house. Make piles sorted by date. Put a Post-it note on the top photo with the year and wrap an elastic band around the piles. Start putting the pictures into albums in chronological order. Pay attention to the photos — how far back do they go? How much has changed? Look how far you've come! Enjoy this personal time to reminisce. The key to happiness is to be thankful for all of the fun you've had with the great people you know.

# Principle #180

## Find your inner musician.

— ✳ —

There are at least 5 good reasons to learn a musical instrument. Studies show that learning to read and play music makes you smarter and helps to prevent or slow down conditions, such as Alzheimer's, that are associated with memory loss. Taking music lessons means you must practice, which ensures that you will have at least an hour or more several times a week to yourself. Playing music reduces stress levels and may even make you laugh as you express yourself in this meaningful way. Once you can play a piece of music from beginning to end, you will feel a great sense of accomplishment.

# PRINCIPLE #181

## Go window shopping.

—————————— ❈ ——————————

Take 20 minutes from your lunch hour or after work and go window shopping. Peer into various shops and pretend you have all the money in the world to spend on yourself. What would you buy? Carry a little notebook and write down a few items you plan to save up for. One study found that 46 percent of people came up with their holiday gift ideas by window shopping.

# PRINCIPLE #182

## Dance around your living room to your favorite song.

Mayo Clinic researchers have concluded that dancing reduces stress, increases energy, improves strength, and increases coordination. Grab a few minutes in the evening to dance to your favorite song. Taking time to move your body when no one is watching frees you from feeling self-conscious. Spending time celebrating your body through movement improves self-esteem and is great exercise.

# Principle #183

## Make a standing date with yourself.

Have date night once a week — with yourself. See a movie one week, go to dinner the next. Visit an art gallery or attend a concert. It may feel awkward at first, but eventually you will not only feel comfortable being out by yourself, you'll look forward to it. You will discover your likes and dislikes through trying different activities. Also, consider how many things you've wanted to do over the years but missed because you could not get your partner or friends to go with you. When you make plans for yourself, you're sure to be in good company. Learning to love being with yourself is key to happiness.

# Principle #184

## Stick to your routine
## when life begins to pile up.

When life gets busy and obligations start to pile up, the first things to go out the window are often the commitments we have with ourselves. But sacrificing time with yourself is unfair and unhealthy. Keep the commitments you make with yourself. Your plans are every bit as important as anyone else's. Sticking to your routine is beneficial to your well-being and crucial to your self-confidence. Think about the kind of message you send when you easily cancel your own plans. When you give up your "me time," you risk stress overload and burnout.

# Principle #185

## Make a new dish — for one.

Cooking for one can be discouraging — who wants to make a whole pan of lasagna and then eat nothing else for a week? If you cook for one, learn new one-serving recipes to make mealtimes enjoyable. Prepare dishes that can be broken down into single servings and then frozen. Most of all, make dining a pleasant experience. Use a nice placemat and a cloth napkin. Sip a glass of wine or sparkling water with dinner and space out the courses. Set a relaxing mood by lighting candles and playing music. Savor each bite and take your time. Enjoy your meal and your great company.

# Maintaining
## a Positive Outlook

People who maintain a positive outlook tend to view life as generally good and regard their failures as learning experiences rather than setbacks. In turn, they tend to be happier and more successful. Winston Churchill once said, "Success is the ability to go from failure to failure without losing your enthusiasm." Indeed, learning to maintain a positive outlook when challenges arise is one of the most important traits of successful people.

Maintain a positive outlook by curbing the tendency to criticize yourself. Self-criticism is rarely useful and can be quite damaging to your ego, self-image, and sense of purpose. Negative self-talk is one of the biggest threats to your happiness. You may not be able to stop disparaging thoughts from entering your mind, but you certainly can control how you respond to them. Do not lend power to thoughts such as "No one will ever love me," or "I will never make enough money." Instead, replace them with positive messages such as "I will meet someone when the time is right" and "I will ask for a raise at my next performance review." Train your brain to think in terms of actions you can take to either cope with or change a situation you don't like. Your outlook will improve as you practice framing life as a series of opportunities rather than obstacles.

Challenging yourself to adopt a more positive outlook will take work, especially at first. But once you insert the following principles into your daily routine, your inclination toward pessimism will likely shift toward optimism. Studies show that optimism is good for your health. According to Dr. Charles L. Raison of the Emory University School of Medicine in Atlanta, "There's growing evidence that, for many medical illnesses, stress and a negative mental state — pessimism, feeling overwhelmed, being burnt out — has a negative affect on immunity." To this end, the following principles will teach you how to look on the bright side — after a while you'll enjoy doing so because it's good for you!

# Principle #186

## Remember the good times to help you through the bad times.

It is important for both mental and physical health to maintain a positive attitude, even when you're faced with daunting challenges. Remembering the good times in your life will help. Holocaust survivor Viktor Frankl wrote a book titled *Man's Search for Meaning* in which he relates how, in the worst days of his captivity in Nazi concentration camps, he was able to find comfort by recalling his happy former life. The positive attitude that results from remembering the good times in this way will boost your mood and your health.

# Principle #187

## Break large jobs into small, manageable tasks.

At times it is hard to stay confident when a giant task is looming over you. Before beginning, break the job down into smaller, more manageable parts. If every corner of your house is an unsightly mess, deal with each room one at a time. If you have been asked to make Thanksgiving dinner, break the meal up and tackle the dishes one by one. Always acknowledge when you have accomplished a task by crossing it off a larger list. Tackling smaller components of a larger goal will keep you feeling motivated, which positively impacts your overall outlook and chances of success.

# Principle #188

## Don't doubt yourself.

Doubting the decisions you've made is a waste of time and negatively affects your self-esteem. Wishy-washy behavior is annoying to the people around you and does nothing to improve your outlook. Tennis player Arthur Ashe once said, "A wise person decides slowly but abides by these decisions." When faced with a decision, gather all the facts, take your time, and make your best decision — and don't look back. Having confidence that you made the best decision with the information you had at the time can prevent you from spiraling into negativity.

# Principle #189

## Surround yourself with supportive people.

When you decide to make positive changes in your life, it can be difficult to stick to your new behaviors if the people around you aren't supportive. Take time to explain to friends and family that you are working toward maintaining a positive outlook and that you would appreciate encouragement. Most of the people in your life who care about you will easily accommodate and even champion the "new you." Your new outlook may even rub off on them!

# PRINCIPLE #190

## Keep in mind that you are what you think.

Mahatma Gandhi once said, "A man is but the product of his thoughts. What he thinks, he becomes." Realize that you are the sum of your thoughts. If you think negative, ugly, unkind thoughts, you are more than likely viewed by others as a negative, ugly, and unkind person. Bringing about real change in your life will require an overhaul in how you think and respond to both internal and external stimuli. Make an effort to respond to annoying or irritating events with a carefree and positive attitude.

# Principle #191

## Encourage positive attitudes in others.

---- ✳ ----

When you notice a friend or loved one responding positively to adversity, point it out. Say, "I was really impressed with how calm you stayed after that guy cut you off." Behavior gets repeated when it is reinforced, in both ourselves and in others. If you take the time to reinforce positive responses in your friends and family, they will feel good about themselves and continue to behave that way.

# Principle #192

## Celebrate the joys of every day.

———————————— ✳ ————————————

The artist Henri Matisse once said, "There are always flowers for those who want to see them." Each day, take note of the things that make you smile or think a positive thought. If your commute is easier than usual, take note and be thankful. Tune in to the radio, and if you hear a song you like, sing along. When you get coffee in the morning, get an extra one for your coworker. Pay attention to how bringing joy to another person makes you feel. Feel good for helping others see the flowers bloom each and every day. Start a "gratitude journal" in which you note each night a few things that happened that day that you are grateful for.

# Principle #193

## Retire your negative habits.

———— ✳ ————

If you had weights around your ankles as you were trying to walk up a flight of stairs, you would take them off once you realized they were slowing you down. Think of negative habits as weights that impede your ability to move forward in life. Negative habits include assuming the worst, nasty self-talk, gossiping, and feelings of jealousy. Remove those weights and commit yourself to living free of the habits that hold you back.

# Principle #194

## Let go of regrets.

How often have you thought, "If only I had done that," or "If only this had happened to me"? Author Mercedes Lackay has written, "If only. Those must be the two saddest words in the world." Indeed, never dwell on what might have happened; focus on what can happen now and move forward. Regret is possibly the most useless emotion because it holds us prisoner to what cannot be undone. So live as best you can, without remorse and regret. Aim to look at the future with a positive outlook.

# PRINCIPLE #195

## Don't feel guilty about doing things you enjoy.

Give yourself permission to have fun at least once every day. Studies show that people who include enjoyable activities in their day live longer and happier lives. An old proverb states, "The mark of a successful man is one that has spent an entire day on the bank of a river without feeling guilty about it." Never feel guilty about enjoying your life. If someone tries to make you feel bad for having a good time, remind yourself they are probably having difficulty enjoying their own life, which is their problem, not yours. Keep your eye on the ultimate prize — your own happiness.

# Principle #196

## Assume that there is a solution to your problem.

Learn to view problems not as roadblocks but as solvable puzzles. There is a solution to every problem. With some patience and research, you will find it. The next time you can't find your keys, take a deep breath and calm down. Odds are they are somewhere within your reach. Remind yourself that even if your keys are at the bottom of the ocean you will be able to get replacements by calling a locksmith.

# Principle #197

## Strive for what is
in between "all or nothing."

When you set out to accomplish something, avoid "all-or-nothing" thinking. Viewing life in terms of extremes may lead to disappointment and possibly to inaction. Learn to be satisfied when the outcome falls somewhere in the middle. Your state of mind will benefit from allowing for a spectrum of outcomes.

# Principle #198

## Practice positive thinking to improve your health.

Studies show that positive thinking has a direct correlation to your health. In one study, researchers at the University of Wisconsin found that negative thinking actually weakens people's immune systems. Participants were asked to think and write about either extremely positive or extremely negative events in their lives. Those asked to recall positive events were sick less often than those who were asked to dwell on negative events over a period of 6 months. Realize the power of positive thinking to promote both mental and physical health.

# Principle #199

## Set the bar where you can reach it.

Boost your enjoyment of life by setting realistic goals. For instance, if you know you would like to buy a new car but your finances are limited, don't set your sights on a Rolls-Royce. Consider a car you can afford that meets your needs, and save for a down payment. You will find that it is easier to reach your goals if you have a friend who will support you by asking about your progress and providing encouragement. Studies show that setting realistic goals and reaching them is one of the most significant ways to dramatically improve one's attitude and maintain a positive outlook.

# Principle #200

## We are all a work in progress.

———————————— ✳ ————————————

Life is an ongoing process of learning, growing, making mistakes, and moving forward through time. No decision you make is final. Every dream can be pursued. Devote yourself to your life. You only get to live it once — live it the very best you can. Consider what Winston Churchill meant when he said, "A pessimist sees the difficulty in every opportunity; an optimist sees the opportunity in every difficulty." By taking the obstacles you encounter as opportunities to grow, learn, and change, you can and will lead a happier life.

# Additional Information and Ideas

The following pages contain a few exercises that will help you enjoy life and be happy. The more you practice these exercises, the more your mood, self-esteem, and outlook on life will improve.

Make a habit of performing these exercises whenever you are feeling sad, lonely, or depressed. These exercises will help you overcome obstacles that are preventing you from being happy. They will also help you appreciate all the good things in your life.

You will find that there are many reasons why you should enjoy life and be happy. Practice these exercises so you can celebrate your past accomplishments, feel fortunate for what you have now, as well as prepare and look forward to new opportunities. If you're already happy, you can use these exercises to help increase your sense of well-being.

These exercises will help you enjoy life and be happy in the following ways:

### Listing Your Accomplishments
Look at how much you've already achieved in life. This is a good way to make yourself feel happy.

### Affirming Yourself
Verbally expressing your positive attributes will help you accept yourself and be happy with who you are.

### Setting Goals
Knowing where you're headed in life and what you have to do to get there is a key to being happy and enjoying life.

## Visualizing Your Success or Happiness

Being happy will be easier if you create something tangible that symbolizes happiness.

## Finding Relaxation

When you decrease stress you are more likely to notice the beauty of the world around you and feel happy as a result.

## Listing Your Accomplishments

Use the categories below to help you articulate your accomplishments. Under each subject list at least three successful attempts or completions. Write your list down in a notebook and carry it around with you. Add to it as needed.

1. Education (college, trade, graduate)
2. Career
3. Home
4. Friendships
5. Romantic relationships
6. Family
7. Hobbies
8. Health
9. Travel
10. Financial
11. Personal growth

## Affirming Yourself

Tell yourself something from this list several times a day. Don't be shy! Look in a mirror if you can while you say it. Focus on the words and how it feels to make positive statements about yourself. When you feel the urge to say "This is stupid," force yourself to replace that thought with one of the affirmations below.

- I am smart
- I am capable
- I am learning
- I am doing my best
- I am a good person
- I am fun
- I am proud of myself
- I love myself
- I forgive myself
- I am good at what I do
- I will succeed
- I am happy
- I am loving

- I am kind
- I am thankful
- I am grateful
- I accept my flaws
- I have many strengths
- I am entitled to happiness
- I deserve to be happy
- I am a work in progress
- I am important
- I like my body
- My body is acceptable
- I respect myself
- I deserve respect from others

## SETTING GOALS

Make a list of your goals. Be sure to include both long- and short-term goals. Make sure to break bigger dreams into smaller, attainable goals. Use the ideas below to help you along. Write in this book and keep it so that you'll always have access to your dreams and goals. Write in pencil and revise when necessary.

My dream is to_____.

These are the steps I can take to turn my dream into a goal:

1.

2.

3.

4.

5.

Things I want to accomplish this year:

1.

2.

3.

4.

5.

Things I want to accomplish this month:

1.

2.

3.

4.

5.

Things I want to accomplish this week:

1.

2.

3.

4.

5.

Things I want to accomplish today:

1.

2.

3.

4.

5.

## Visualizing Your Success or Happiness

Make your internal ideas external. Take some time to do the following visualization and realization exercises. Creating something tangible from your imagination will help you to realize your dreams.

- Write yourself a check for a million dollars and hang it on your bathroom mirror. This exercise works on many levels. It encourages you to work hard to increase your financial wealth; it is a constant reminder that you are highly valuable, and it gives you a sense of power to see your name next to the words "one million dollars." Using a real check makes it a real possibility.

- Keep a constant list of things you enjoy. Each time you smile, write down what you were thinking or what happened to bring you that moment of joy. Note when you feel completely happy and describe it in detail. Pay attention to the stimuli and feelings. Be curious about what brings you joy and seek more of it. Review this list once a week and allow yourself to reexperience the joy from the previous week.

- Get some canvases and paints. It doesn't matter if you are not artistically inclined. If you can write, you can do this exercise. Pick a few words that mean something to you, such as *love, success, joy, happiness,* or *peace.* Choose a color that best matches what that word feels like to you. Paint the word on one of the canvases. If you're feeling creative, fill the canvas with whatever you're inspired to paint. Hang your creative expressions around your home to enhance your environment and remind you of what matters most to you.

# Finding Relaxation

1.  Inhale and exhale deeply and very slowly 10 times.
2.  Stretch your back and legs by reaching to your toes with your fingers without bending your knees. Go as far down as you can.
3.  Lie flat on your back. Extend your arms overhead and keep your legs straight. Reach through your fingertips and toes in opposite directions. Hold for 5 seconds and then relax.
4.  Start from your shoulders and progressively relax each muscle group by stretching and releasing tension, ending with your toes.
5.  Take a warm bath
6.  Get a massage
7.  Light candles
8.  Drink a cup of chamomile tea
9.  Massage your own scalp

10. Close your eyes for 10 minutes during the day and think positive thoughts.
11. Exercise for at least 30 minutes each day
12. Practice yoga
13. Practice tai chi
14. Go for a walk in the sunshine
15. Use aromatherapy
16. Listen to soothing music
17. Meditate
18. Get enough sleep

# Conclusion

**Congratulations!** After reading this book you should feel excited about your prospects for increased happiness in your life. This book has illustrated the main reasons why people with very little can be very happy, while others with much more are very tense and unhappy. As the principles herein have demonstrated, happiness is always within reach. All you really need is a positive attitude.

Happiness is a state of mind. We all know that sadness, disappointment, and setbacks are a part of life. But you don't need to let these situations keep you down. The secret is to focus on what you have versus what you don't have and to look forward to the opportunities that lie ahead of you.

The simple principles presented in this book will make a real difference in how you feel. If you apply these principles on a regular basis, you will feel happier. It is not enough to read this book one time. You need to read it several times the first month and then at least once every month until you find yourself applying many of the principles illustrated in this book on a daily basis.

Studies show that it takes approximately 30 days for a behavior to become a habit. Spend extra time during the first month practicing positive thoughts and behaviors until it becomes second nature for you. You will soon find yourself enjoying your life and being much happier than you ever thought possible.

There is a happier life ahead of you if you open yourself up to the positive and proactive ways of thinking presented in this book. Remember, you can be happy, you deserve to be happy and, from this day forward, you will be happy!